SINGLE MOTHERS BY CHOICE

onsidering the joys and responsi-
this book is invaluable. It should
amine their options realistically
ision. It doesn't proselytize and
best sense of the word, a true

of pediatric psychology at New

hoice, I found this book to be
ovoking advice it provides and
thers that are shared in it. As a
nd the book a well-written and
otion of single parenthood."
rsity of South Alabama

elighted we have a book that can
swer our questions—even those
et, but will need to. Ms. Mattes'
ghly and seriously without being
iff and formal.
talking with a very good friend.
an who is either thinking about
"

University Northwest

SINGLE MOTHERS BY CHOICE

A Guidebook for Single
Women Who Are Considering
or Have Chosen Motherhood

JANE MATTES L.C.S.W.

THREE RIVERS PRESS • NEW YORK

Copyright © 1994, 1997 by Jane Mattes

Published by Three Rivers Press, New York, New York.
Member of the Crown Publishing Group.

Random House, Inc. New York, Toronto, London, Sydney, Auckland
www.randomhouse.com

THREE RIVERS PRESS is a registered trademark and the Three Rivers Press
colophon is a trademark of Random House, Inc.

Originally published by Times Books in 1994 and 1997.

Printed in the United States of America

Design by Jo Anne Metsch

Library of Congress Cataloging-in-Publication Data
Mattes, Jane.
Single mothers by choice / by Jane Mattes.—1st ed.
Includes bibliographical references and index.
1. Unmarried mothers—United States—Case studies. 2. Single mothers—United
States—Case studies. 3. Single Mothers by Choice (Organization). I. Title.
HQ759.45.M37   1994   306.85'6—dc20   94-13460

ISBN 978-0-8129-2246-2

*This book is dedicated to
my son, Eric.*

CONTENTS

ACKNOWLEDGMENTS

This book could not have been written at all without the help of the many, many wonderful members of Single Mothers by Choice, who were willing to discuss their innermost thoughts and their doubts, fears, and triumphs about single motherhood. To all these women—thank you for having been courageous and open enough to explore your own feelings, and then to share them with me.

My agent, Leslie Breed, was committed to and pursued this project with unrelenting dedication and enthusiasm, and I thank her for her unwavering faith in the value of the book.

Susanna Porter, my editor at Times Books, was a pleasure to work with and consistently gave me inspiration and support. Her suggestions were always made with great respect and sensitivity, which helped make the editing process a real pleasure.

A big thank-you to my mother, Hilda Mattes, who, with never-ending devotion, was always available to help me care for my son, and who has been there with love and patience for us through thick and thin.

My son, Eric, of course, made all this possible, and I am especially grateful to have been fortunate enough to be his mother. But he deserves special thanks for his amazing patience and understanding during the seemingly endless hours I had to spend at the computer while working on this book.

Longtime friends Ann and Ira Bindman gave of themselves with enormous generosity of spirit—way above and beyond the call of friendship—for which I am very grateful.

Attorney Rebecca Rawson was kind enough to read the manuscript from the legal point of view. Her comments invariably were both helpful and supportive. And Andrea Troy, adoption specialist, made invaluable contributions to the chapter on single-parent adoption.

Thanks also go to Dr. Chaim Shatan and Dr. Arthur Robbins, both of whom encouraged me to follow my own path and helped me find the courage to do so. Similarly, many friends and colleagues listened to and nurtured me as I went through the lengthy process of writing this book—especially Susan Berlin and Susan Anderson and the group—Diane, Fred, Joel, Judy, Lois, Mary, Nancy, and Rick.

NEW RESOURCES AVAILABLE FROM SMC

SMC (Single Mothers by Choice) is on the Internet! Information about our services, as well as some articles from past issues of our newsletter, can be found at www.single mothersbychoice.com.

SMC also has a private listserv for our members so we can provide virtual support to one another via e-mail.

Lastly, we now have a Sibling Registry available so parents can register children conceived through donor insemination and learn if there are any half-siblings (children of the same donor) registered with us. If we have mutual consent, we will notify the parents when we find a match.

INTRODUCTION

When I first decided that I would have a baby as a single woman, I was so nervous about my decision that I had nightmares in which outraged people threw stones at me. In my slightly more realistic moments I simply feared that my career as a psychotherapist would be ruined and that I would be ousted by the psychoanalytic society at which I had trained; that my family would disown me or refuse to have anything to do with my child and me; and that my friends would refuse to support or help me and would respond to my times of distress by saying that I had chosen to do this alone and I had no right to expect help from anyone.

My guilt was palpable. I was doing something that I considered forbidden and I felt I would be lucky to escape with only minor injuries—emotional, if not physical. I had been raised in a traditional family in which the predominant value system was "What will people think?" and I had always assumed that I would have to be married in order to have a baby. As a matter of fact, my first professional job after receiving my master's degree in social work was at a "residence" for unwed mothers, a place where unmarried teen-aged girls were sent to hide their pregnancies (in order to spare themselves and their families the shame of exposure) prior to giving up their babies to married couples for adoption. This was in 1966.

Could I now, in 1979, turn around and do exactly what I had always thought to be unacceptable? Well, as it turned out, I could. And I did. I was thirty-six, I had established a thriving private practice in psychotherapy, I was the director of a psychotherapy clinic, and I was teaching and supervising at a training institute—I had accomplished just about all of my professional goals. However, I had not been able to find a suitable life partner and I realized that I did not have much time left in which to start a family.

Thinking that I could get married at any age, I decided to postpone the search for a husband and look into adopting a baby first. To my surprise, when I told friends and family about my plan, they all urged me to try to conceive rather than adopt. I wasn't sure that I would feel comfortable in the role of "unmarried mother," but while looking into various adoption resources I accidentally conceived with a lover whom I had known for several years—and my ambivalence disappeared. I don't know if it was the effect of the hormones or if I had really wanted this all along and hadn't been quite able to admit it to myself, but I was totally thrilled.

My lover had always been very candid about the fact that he was not interested in marriage or family, so I was not surprised that he wanted no involvement as a parent. I left the door open for him to change his mind at any point, and he wished me good luck. I was clear that I would be raising my child alone, as I had been considering, but it would be my biological child rather than an adopted one. In August of 1980 my son, Eric, was born. And so I began the most exciting adventure I have ever undertaken.

After having gone through the long and rigorous training required to become a psychoanalyst, I felt sure that nothing could be as hard as that. I was wrong—being the mother of a newborn was, for me, much harder. I needed support, but at first I was too proud to ask for it. However, people kept telling me about their acquaintances, single women who were either pregnant or thinking about becoming pregnant or adopting, and I decided that I would try to organize these people and form a small support group for myself. I also thought that it would be good for my son to get to know other children who were growing up without knowing their fathers.

I arbitrarily picked a date and told literally everyone I knew that if they knew of anyone who was single and had decided to have a baby or who was even contemplating it, they should tell her that I was having an informal get-together at my house at this time and date. I had no idea who or how many women would turn up, and when the designated time came I was amazed to find that eight women were in my living room! Two had tiny babies, a few months younger than my then eleven-month-old son, and several were in various stages of pregnancy. There also were a few women who were thinking about becoming single mothers by choice.

We started chatting and couldn't stop. It quickly became apparent that we had a bond that drew us together and so we decided to meet again. At the next meeting we once again found that it was a great relief to talk to others in the same situation. We all felt to some extent that we were less comfortable talking with married mothers because we were worried that they would perceive us as complainers. We feared that married mothers in particular would not be supportive and might even be critical of us for taking on single parenting when we couldn't handle it perfectly. I feared I might be told, "Well, what did you *expect*?" Since we had done something controversial, we felt we had to show people that we could deal with it without difficulty. But with one another we were able to be totally honest.

We talked about the wonderful times, which turned out to be the most poignant ones, since none of us had anyone who loved and cared about our babies as much as we did. And we talked, and eventually laughed, about the tough times—the stupid things we did until we learned better, the mistakes we made until we found the solutions we needed. We had not realized how hungry we were to talk openly to other single mothers like ourselves, and our spirits and social lives improved as we arranged to meet one another on weekends. We had all found that often couples with children preferred to get together with other couples on weekends, and spending two full days alone with a small baby could be quite lonely.

We also brainstormed for answers to common problems like how to get to the store when the baby is sick and you are not supposed to take her out but you can't leave her home alone. We compared notes on how we responded when strangers asked us, as they always seemed to, what were our husbands' reactions to the baby, and laughed as we discussed some of the things we felt like replying at times. And we talked about the ways in which we felt we had an easier time of it than married women: we didn't have to keep the house and ourselves all together, and we didn't have to worry about anyone else besides the baby. It was wonderful to meet and talk with other women who shared so many of the same feelings and experiences as mine.

During one of our early meetings one of the women in our group asked us if we would mind if a friend of hers, who worked for a local New York City newspaper, wrote an article about our group. We all agreed and several weeks later an article appeared in the New York *Daily News* about our get-togethers. The article attracted calls and letters from about thirty women, asking if they could attend. We set about finding a larger meeting space than my living room and happily expanded our group.

Not too long after this first article appeared, an award-winning reporter from *The New York Times* contacted us and asked to interview us. This article proved to be the turning point in our becoming a national organization as it was not only printed in *The New York Times* but also syndicated in newspapers all across the country. Suddenly we were deluged with mail and phone calls requesting information, support, anything we could offer. We spent hours of our precious free time talking to people from many different states, and soon realized we would have to get more orgamized. We appointed officers, turned a lot of work over to the women who did not yet have babies (they had free time and we didn't), and became a nonprofit corporation in 1982, a year after my first living-room gathering.

One of our lengthiest discussions involved what we should name the organization. We felt strongly that we wanted the name to clearly convey that is was our choice and our decision to become single mothers, unlike divorced or widowed mothers. (Some of us made the choice before conceiving, and some, like me, decided after having conceived, but we all chose motherhood at some point.) There was no name that slid trippingly across the tongue, but we finally settled on "Single Mothers by Choice" as the one that best described us: single women who *chose* to become mothers; single mothers who are mature and responsible and who feel empowered rather than victimized. The acronym SMC is used by many of our members, and as the organization has spread throughout the country people are starting to recognize what it stands for.

Eventually we had enough members in various parts of the

United States to begin putting them in touch with one another, and in time they formed local chapters. Our membership grew slowly but surely until 1992, when then Vice Presidemt Quayle decided to attack the TV character Murphy Brown for not having good family values. Thanks to his decision to make an issue about single motherhood, we were flooded with media attention, and requests for information about our group tripled. As of this writing, there are about two thousand members and more than twenty local Single Mothers by Choice chapters in the United States and one in Canada, with new chapters continuing to form. There clearly was and is a need out there for such a group.

Since that first informal get-together in my living room in 1981 I have given many workshops in various parts of the country and met hundreds of SMCs and also those we call "thinkers"—women who are *considering* single motherhood. The "thinkers" comprise almost half of our membership, as women are growing increasingly aware that single motherhood is a real option—but that the decision warrants considerable thought. In many chapters of Single Mothers by Choice, "thinkers" meet together and spend months deciding whether or not single motherhood is right for them. About 50 percent of our "thinkers" decide *not* to become single mothers—but it is as important for them to have gone through the decision-making process and made a careful choice about single motherhood as it is for women who opt to try it.

I have learned a great deal from our members, as well as from the many individual SMCs whom I have counseled in my private practice and of course also from raising my own son, who is now an adult. I have been especially interested in understanding more about the issues associated with children being raised without a father. There are many variables, whether the pregnancy was planned or unplanned, for example, makes a difference in how the mother and the children adjust to the situation.

This book is an attempt to share some of what I have learned from all these personal and professional experiences, with the hope that it can be of use to others. It has not been an easy journey, but it has been a most fulfilling and enlightening one.

These days, my son bears little resemblance to the baby I held in my arms at that first mothers' get-together. He has been working and living on his own since graduating from college, and is now attending graduate school. Everyone asks me, "How did he turn out?" The answer: just fine. He is smart, loving, and talented, and I am very proud of him (and maybe just a tad prejudiced). He has brought me great joy and taught me a lot, particularly about patience and acceptance and love. I am very grateful for the opportunity to have raised him.

Special Note to the Reader: As it is cumbersome to write "he or she" all the time if one wants to avoid using the male singular pronoun to refer to both sexes, I have tried to alternate the use of he and she in a balanced way throughout the text.

PART ONE

Making the Decision
and
Carrying It Out

PART ONE

Making the Decision
and
Carrying It Out

1

. . . .

WHO IS THE
SINGLE MOTHER BY CHOICE?

When Alice, a manager in a medical supplies business, decided to become a single mother, she was thirty-six. She had been in several fairly serious relationships in her twenties and early thirties but had not felt ready to commit to a marriage. By her mid-thirties she had accomplished most of her career goals and she recognized that it was time to focus on her personal goals and try to find "Mr. Right." But as she looked for someone to settle down with, she found that most of the men in her age range who were interested in getting married and having a family had already done so. She realized that it might not be so easy to find a spouse. She very much wanted to have a family and so began to consider whether or not she could become a single mother.

Alice felt confident that she had the capacity to be a good parent and knew that she could afford to support a child. Her family and friends were people she felt she could depend on for emotional support (and maybe even for a little baby-sitting help). So she did some research at the library and found out about Single Mothers by Choice. She wrote to us and requested our literature. We put her in touch with the organization's local chapter.

There she met and talked with several single women who were already mothers and some others who were thinking about becoming mothers either through donor insemination or with a sex partner or by adoption.

After several months of talking with women from the group and with several close friends, Alice decided that donor insemination was the route she felt most comfortable taking. She went to her gynecologist and told him of her decision. He was supportive, and after some preliminary medical tests, Alice began the process of donor insemination. About sixteen months after her initial visit to the doctor, Alice was the proud mother of a baby girl.

A single mother by choice is a woman who starts out raising her child without a partner. She may or may not marry later on, but at the outset she is parenting alone. This definition excludes unmarried couples, heterosexual or homosexual, because although they are not legally married, they will be coparenting, and it also excludes women who became mothers while they were married and then later were widowed or divorced.

IS SINGLE MOTHERHOOD RIGHT FOR YOU?

Following this chapter, there is a questionnaire that will help you focus your thinking and clarify the issues you might need to address as you decide whether or not to become a single mother by choice.

How do you decide? Most of us were raised with the dream of falling in love with a wonderful man, getting married, and raising a child in a loving relationship. To be happy being an SMC you need to come to terms with giving up your dream of parenting a child from the beginning with a loving partner. Perhaps you will get married in the future, perhaps you won't. You may decide to have a child but may never get married, or you may decide not to have a child and try harder to find a mate, only to end up having neither. There are no guarantees.

When trying to make the decision, keep in mind that your choice will affect the course of your life in a profound way. It is therefore a very major decision and one that shouldn't be made in haste or on impulse. A feeling of loneliness around the end-of-year holidays may make you yearn for a family of your own, but how do you feel during the rest of the year? If you cherish your freedom and independence most of the time, then be aware that those yearnings may just be seasonal.

When you fantasize about having a baby, do you picture a specific baby? What are the characteristics of this baby? Is it a boy or girl? How old is it? What kind of situation are you picturing? Is the baby cuddled in your arms or playing by itself? Is it awake or asleep? Is it crying or smiling? What kind of temperament does it have? Can you picture it at a less adorable moment or at an older age? What do you feel when you imagine it as a toddler and then as a school-age child? And as a teenager?

Do you realize that the baby you give birth to or adopt may be nothing like the baby you imagine having? You have little or no control over the sex, temperament, and personality of your child, and you may or may not be fortunate enough to get the baby of your dreams. What if your baby turns out not to be that baby? What if it has a birth defect or a learning disability? Can you imagine stretching yourself to be able to love it anyway? If you feel you can only love a baby who meets the profile of your ideal baby, you may turn out to be a very disappointed mother if your ideal baby is not the one you end up with. While this happens in two-parent families also, in that situation the child has double the probability that one of the parents will be a natural "fit" for him. When you are the only parent, you may have to work harder to find a way to adapt to who your child is, since you are his primary source of security and nurturing.

Do you have adequate resources to support both yourself and a child? You can raise a child alone without being wealthy, but you need to be prepared for the necessary expenses that come with a child, such as diapers, day care, clothes, recreational supplies and activities, and also the less essential ones like braces, summer camp, a private school, dance classes, or tennis lessons. You will need to put aside money for vacations, emergencies, and ultimately for college. How able are you to commit your emotional and financial resources to a child? What other demands are there on your income? Some of us fall into what is called the "sandwich" generation, caught between taking care of elderly parents while still raising small children of our own. If you have elderly parents, will you be called upon to help them cope with their lives in the next few years, or are there other members of the family who will (or can be persuaded to) take on that responsibility? If your parents need your hands-on help on a daily or weekly basis or need your financial help, either one will take away from your ability to care for your child.

If your work requires a twenty-four-hour-a-day involvement, how would you feel about changing careers or jobs? Would it be a relief to have a less pressured situation or would you feel a great loss? If you want a child but will rarely be home during the child's waking hours, is that the way you want to raise a child?

Judith

Judith, a banker in a large city in Massachusetts, realized that at forty she was at the point where it was now or never to have a baby. She was very close to two of her friends' children, but was aware that it would be more fulfilling to have children of her own. She had been ignoring the little voice that occasionally reminded her that time was running out, but in her late thirties she could not ignore it anymore and she enrolled in a workshop given by Single Mothers by Choice for women who were considering single motherhood.

Although she gave the matter a great deal of thought over the next year, Judith was unable to reach a decision. She was the only child of parents in their seventies and was concerned that they would need her more and more as they continued to age. On the other hand, she felt that she wanted to have a baby and be a mother before it was too late.

Feeling stuck, Judith then decided to attend a group I ran for "thinkers" who are unable to come to a decision after thinking about it for more than a year (we call them "stuck thinkers"). Along with several other women, Judith explained and explored her dilemma. As we talked, it became clear that this was a kind of midlife crisis for Judith. She was beginning the second half of her life and she felt that in the first half she had been too devoted to meeting the needs of others. Now she wanted to do something major for herself, yet she felt that her parents' need for her help in the near future was something she could not ignore.

As she went into more detail about her fantasies, she described how she imagined she would have a baby and move to a house in the country, away from the city but close enough that she could easily commute to her job. She had always wanted a house in the country, she said, with lots of space and a fireplace, and she knew her dog would love it also. I asked her if getting the house had to be connected with a baby, and she said that it did, that she had never thought of having one just for herself. The other women in the group were quick to ask why not, and it was at that point that Judith realized that what she really wanted was a house in the country, and that she had needlessly linked that with first having a baby. In the last few sessions of the group she worked on her sadness about giving up the idea of being a mother and grieved for the child that might never be hers. Then, having given herself permission to fulfill her desire to move to the country, that is what she did, and the last I heard from her she had come to terms with not having a child and was happily living there with her dog.

Single motherhood by choice is an adventure through relatively uncharted territory. It is not for everyone and there are many things you need to consider when making this choice. But most of all, *make a decision.* The worst thing you can do is not think about the issue at all and not make a decision or just keep putting it off. You may then, like Sleeping Beauty, wake up one day, only to discover that Prince Charming never came! You may wish you had gone on with your life instead of waiting for him.

Some women think they have until their forties to decide about motherhood because of all the medical technology available today and so postpone thinking about it, only to realize at forty-two or forty-three that they are very unsure and unclear—and they may also have serious fertility problems by that time. It is an important decision and you owe it to yourself to devote some time and energy to thinking it through before your mid-thirties. Perhaps you will decide at age thirty-two that you want to become a single mother if you have not met a potential mate by age thirty-six. Just knowing that you have made that decision can help you feel better as you are going through your thirties. On the other hand, it is also possible that you might give it extensive thought and, like Judith, decide that single motherhood is not right for you. In that case, you will be clear about your choice and not have to panic at forty-something when you realize you haven't really given it the consideration it deserves.

Whatever decision you ultimately come to, be prepared to find your feelings vacillating along the way. It isn't unusual to change your mind several times during the decision-making phase before you reach a final decision. This does not mean that you are a wishy-washy or indecisive person. In fact, the more you can allow yourself to go through a variety of emotions, the more sure you will be about your decision at the end since you will have examined your feelings from several different points of view.

DEMOGRAPHICS

There has been a dramatic increase in the number of mature single women, and particularly single white women, becoming mothers. The U.S. Census Bureau reported in 1993 that nearly a quarter of the nation's never-married women now become mothers, an increase of 60 percent in the last decade. The increase was particularly sharp among educated and professional women: among white women and women who attended college the percentage more than doubled, and for women with professional or managerial jobs it nearly tripled. The number of single women who have become mothers is actually even higher when you take into consideration that the census report only counted never-married mothers, leaving out the many divorced and widowed women who went on to have children after their marriages ended. These women represent as much as a third of the national membership of Single Mothers by Choice.

More than 209,000 single women over thirty gave birth in 1994, the most recent year for which figures are available. While women of all ethnic backgrounds are choosing to become single mothers, the most dramatic increase in numbers has been among white women. In the ten years between 1980 and 1990 the birth rate for white unmarried mothers between thirty and thirty-four years of age increased 120 percent, while during the same period the rate for black unmarried women in this age group was up only 28 percent. (It is difficult to ascertain the rate of increase for Hispanic women since they may be classified in either the white or black category.) For unmarried white women between thirty-five and thirty-nine years old the birth rate increased by 78 percent from 1980 to 1990 and for those forty to forty-four years old there has been an increase of 38 percent during the same ten years. (Statistics are from the U.S. Public Health Service.)

A study of the mothers in Single Mothers by Choice indicates that most of us are in our mid-thirties and are very concerned about the ticking of our biological clocks when we decide to become single mothers. We are well educated and financially secure, with incomes ranging from a low of $20,000 to a high of over $100,000 a year. Another study of members of our national SMC organization indicates that the median income of our members is $42,000 per year, higher than that of the average man in the United States (median income of the average man was about $23,000 as reported by *U.S. News and World Report* in 1991) so we are at least as able, if not more able, to support a child and ourselves as is the average man. More than half of us have attended college and many have postgraduate degrees, and our careers are in fields such as medicine, banking, mental health, the arts, law, business, communications, the sciences, and education. Some of us are self-employed and own our own businesses.*

We often plan for a baby for several years, just as many married couples do, putting aside a portion of our earnings, buying a house in a neighborhood within a good school district, sometimes even changing jobs or careers in order to have a more flexible schedule or do less traveling or attend fewer evening meetings in order to be able to spend more time with our baby.

Some SMCs have never been married, others were divorced or widowed before becoming mothers. We come from a variety of ethnic and religious backgrounds, and our social and political beliefs cover a wide range from conservative to traditional.† We are predominantly heterosexual (possibly because most lesbian mothers are parenting in couples), but we include both straight and gay women in our numbers. Some of us are financially well-off and others are struggling to make ends meet. In other words, we represent a real cross section of women in this country. The one thing we all have in common is the desire to be a mother and the belief that one loving parent can do a good job of raising a child.

*Ciborowski, Paul, and Jane Mattes. "Single Mothers by Choice: SMC 2000 Study Report No. 1," published in the Single Mothers by Choice newsletter, September 1991.

†Bryant, Lori, and Patricia Willems. "Single Mothers by Choice: Traditional Values and Maternal Role Satisfaction," Master of Social Welfare, UCLA, 1990.

WHY IS THIS HAPPENING?

There are probably a number of reasons for the increase in older single women having babies, but I believe that the one that underlies them all is the women's movement. By refusing to accept the premise that all women should find their fulfillment solely within the family as wives and mothers, and by identifying and fighting for women's rights, the women's movement has made it possible for women today to have choices. We can have satisfying careers out of the home, or we can stay home and raise a family, or both. Whichever path we choose, we have a better sense of self-esteem and feel more empowered than ever before. The days when a woman had to be married to feel that she could have a rewarding and satisfying life are long over, and women who do not marry have many other ways to find fulfillment.

Until the women's movement, women were often regarded as perpetual children ("girls") who were incapable of dealing with the world without the support and protection of men. This was (and often still is) symbolized by the woman's father "giving away" his daughter to her future husband at her wedding. In most cases marriage was not seen as a partnership, but as an agreement that a man would take care of a woman in exchange for her agreeing to submit to his authority. Men made the major decisions and were the disciplinarians. They were the sole support of the family and their wives were totally dependent upon them, almost like one of the children.

This position was typified by the threat to the child, "Wait until your father gets home!" or, alternatively, the plea to the child, "Don't tell your father that I bought this dress." Thanks in great part to the women's movement, many of us now feel capable of running countries and businesses, not to mention being heads of households. We are not only financially more able to support a family, but also feel more capable of being a good parent and raising a child, even raising a child alone. We may be interested in marriage to a man whom we feel would be a loving partner, but we do not need, nor are we willing, to marry a man who is not right for us solely in order to have a child, particularly in light of the fact that so many marriages in recent years have been ending in divorce.

Because of the high rate of divorce we have all seen women who had not planned or been prepared to take on the responsibility of being single parents being forced to do so. In many cases they have managed to develop the skills necessary to cope with the job. It is not surprising, then, that a mature single woman would feel that if she *decides* to become a single mother she can do at least as well as, if not better than, someone who was unexpectedly left with the task at the end of a bad marriage and an upsetting, life-disrupting divorce.

It is no longer the case that if a woman doesn't marry she is considered an "old maid" with no other sources of satisfaction in her life. Not that long ago, an unmarried woman was an object of pity, seen as a "nothing" or a "nobody" unless she was legally attached to a man. Women routinely were (and sometimes still are) addressed as "Mrs. John Smith" rather than Mary Smith because Mary Smith was not seen as an interesting person in her own right. Today a woman who is not married can have a successful and rewarding career, she can have a social and sexual life, and she can have a family by adopting or conceiving a baby. Marriage is not her only path to happiness.

PERSONALITY

Some women have an easier time dealing with the stresses of single motherhood than others. For example, if you are a flexible person who accepts and enjoys differences among people, you are more likely to feel fairly comfortable with a family structure that is atypical, or what is often called an "alternative" family. On the other hand, if you have very definite ideas about right and wrong or good and bad, you might find that you are not as comfortable with choosing an unconventional path. In order to help your future child feel good about being part of an alternative family, you will have to be able to present the concept of being different in a positive light. If you believe that differences are not a good thing, that there really is only one right way to do things, you will have a hard time conveying to your child that coming from an alternative kind of family is really fine.

It certainly helps if you can maintain your equilibrium and your self-esteem without a great deal of external support, since our society is not wholly supportive of single mothers by choice (and may never be). You may wish that your choice was applauded by all, but in fact you don't really need universal support if you have the courage of your own convictions. You really only need a few significant people to understand and be supportive. (More on the need for support systems later.)

If you are very determined to become a single mother you will, not surprisingly, find it easier to cope with the stresses than if you are ambivalent about it. If you plan your pregnancy and very much want your baby, the accomplishment of your goal is in and of itself a great satisfaction and you will have an easier adjustment to motherhood. If, however, you accidentally become pregnant or have very mixed feelings about whether or not to become a single mother, you will probably find the subsequent adjustment to single motherhood more difficult.

A good support system is crucial for an SMC, particularly in the earliest stages of motherhood. Some people are more comfortable establishing such a system, while others find it very difficult to reach out and ask for help when in a stressful situation. Where do you fall in this spectrum? Can you let people know that you need help and accept it from them relatively comfortably? If so, you can probably succeed in raising your baby within a network of people who care about both of you, and as a result you will feel less alone. If you were married, your husband would ideally be your primary support system, but since you do not have a spouse, you can and should divide the support function among several people.

STIGMA

There has been a significant lessening of the stigma that was formerly associated with out-of-wedlock births. By the late seventies, three fourths of Americans surveyed said that it was not morally wrong for a woman to have a child outside of a marriage. A poll taken by *Glamour* magazine in 1986 indicated that 77 percent of its readers (primarily women in their twenties and thirties) approved of single women choosing to have children and 70 percent would consider having a child outside of marriage if they were not married by their mid-thirties.

Despite denouncements by then Vice President Quayle, the *Murphy Brown* TV show was number one in the ratings the week that television's first single mother by choice gave birth to her out-of-wedlock child (and for many weeks prior to and after that). *Thirty-four million* viewers watched that episode of the show! While in the past such a plot development might have led to angry sponsors protesting or canceling their commercials, none did in this case. Quite the contrary: the star, Candice Bergen, was on the cover of several national magazines and both Ms. Bergen and the show received Emmy awards.

Clearly, public opinion has changed since Ingrid Bergman was ostracized by Hollywood in 1952 for giving birth to famed director Roberto Rossellini's child when she was not married to him. In fact, the decrease in stigma has been so apparent that in a recent article in *The Atlantic*, the author urged a return to stigmatizing single mothers because she was concerned about the increase in single-parent homes and worried that the children of such homes are more likely to have problems than those in intact families.* Research has indicated, however, that it is the stability and lack of disruption in the home, rather than the number of parents, that has the major impact on the child's adjustment. Teen-aged children of never-married mothers evaluated in a 1992 study have been shown to have a better adjustment than those from either divorced homes or stepfamilies, despite the fact that overall the divorced and stepparent families had higher incomes.†

I personally have seen a dramatic change in attitudes during the thirteen years since I had my son, although there are still many misunderstandings and much confusion about who we are. As the national spokesperson for Single Mothers by Choice, I have been interviewed on numerous TV and radio

---

*Dafoe Whitehead, Barbara. "Dan Quayle Was Right." *The Atlantic*, May 1993, pp. 47–84.
†Demo, David, and Charles Acock. "Family Structure and Adolescent Behavior," paper presented at the annual meeting of the American Sociological Association, August 1992.

shows, as well as for many magazines and newspapers. In the first few years of doing these interviews, I was often asked questions that reflected not only a prejudice against us, but almost a total distortion of what we were all about—questions like why did SMCs hate men or why were we against the idea of family. I would try to explain that, to the contrary, we were trying to create families in the best way that we could and that most of us would have preferred to do so in the traditional way with a loving partner. My clarifications appeared to fall on deaf ears. The interviewers seemed to have a fixed idea that we must be man-haters or, at the least, radical feminists who were trying to overthrow the traditional American family structure.

In recent interviews, I am happy to say, I have rarely been asked these kinds of questions. Today the interviewers are more positive but, like so many people in the general population, they are still confused about how an SMC differs from other kinds of single mothers. They often mistakenly equate us with divorced or teen-aged single mothers. Occasionally they (incorrectly) assume that the "choice" part of single mother by choice refers to our unmarried state, rather than to the choice of becoming a mother. In asking about the effect the absence of a father has on the children, they sometimes (erroneously) assume that our children must have been traumatized by a rejection or abandonment by their fathers, or they point to studies about children from "broken homes," confusing our families with divorced families. Our homes have not been broken, and our children have not experienced any such trauma. But, for the most part, the interviewers now seem to be more aware that we are mature women who simply wanted to be mothers before it was too late. Some actually see us as courageous women who are dedicated mothers. On the whole, the questions asked these days often seem to reflect more of a desire to understand the single-mother-by-choice phenomenon rather than an attack on our motivations or value systems.

WILL THERE BE PSYCHOLOGICAL DAMAGE TO THE CHILDREN?

My field, the mental-health field, has for many years been concerned about the effects on children of stresses such as poverty and disruptions in the family such as divorce and abandonment. Often when I appear on a panel or TV show discussing single mothers by choice with some of my fellow psychotherapists or child development experts, they lump single-mothers-by-choice families into the same category as families who have experienced these kinds of stresses. They warn of the likelihood of behavioral problems (criminal and violent behavior), problems in learning, and problems with relationships, among others. However, as they have become more aware that the SMC's child has *not* experienced the loss of a parent or the breakup and disruption of a family, the professionals have recently sounded more positive about the future of the SMC children. In fact, when I was on a television program recently, the psychologist who had been brought on the show to debate me actually leaped out of his chair to defend SMCs against what he felt were unfair criticisms!

A study mentioned earlier, from the University of Missouri department of human development and family studies, brings some good news. The authors found that adolescents whose mothers had never married have fewer conflicts with their parents, better school grades, and fewer personal and adjustment problems than children from either divorced or step-parent families.* The population of never-married mothers

*Demo and Acock. "Family Structure and Adolescent Behavior."

used in this study was for the most part fairly young and financially disadvantaged, while the divorced and stepfamily parents were older and had higher incomes, and yet the children of the never-married mothers still were reported to have a better adjustment than those who had experienced more family disruption. This study highlights the importance of differentiating between various kinds of single-parent homes when we talk about the impact of single-parent homes on the children: were the homes disrupted by divorce and/or remarriage or were they stable? It seems to me, and makes common sense as well, that the crucial matter is that the child feels secure, loved, and wanted and that there be minimal family disruption—not whether she is raised by one parent or two. Most experts in child development now say cautiously that it is too soon to be sure, but it appears that the children of SMCs have as good a chance of turning out well as any other child.

On another occasion when I was a speaker on a panel about single mothers by choice at a national Jewish organization, I was warned to be prepared for strong criticism from the rabbi who was also on the panel. I sat waiting nervously, but when it was the rabbi's turn to speak, there was no criticism at all. To the contrary, and to the surprise of many in the room, she applauded single mothers for trying to create and raise a family and carry on the traditional role of Jewish women as devoted and loving mothers! I was first relieved and then somewhat amused as she gently scolded the audience for not doing enough to "help these women find husbands."

I think that we need to keep in mind that we are living in changing times, and that the so-called "alternative family" (stepparent family, single-parent family, and gay or lesbian or heterosexual couple living together) is now more common than the traditional family. We all surely would agree that having a child in a family with two loving parents is the ideal situation, but after many years of overidealizing the traditional family, we now also know that it was not perfect. The fact that children can be raised successfully in other kinds of families is becoming more accepted. I believe that our energies would be best invested in trying to learn more about what things work in *all* families, both traditional and alternative ones, where the children turn out well, rather than continuing to be fearful of change and insisting that alternative families cannot work.

FINANCES

Life is certainly easier if you have a lot of money. This is also true for single motherhood, which can be much more stressful if a tight money situation is causing there to be additional pressure on the mother. Money can make it easier for you to give yourself some nurturing, which can make all the difference when you are trying to maintain your equilibrium and patience with your child. However, there are substitutes for money in the life of a single mother—a good support system is priceless and also free. Money can buy baby-sitters, vacations, massages, and other tangible things, but single mothers with good support systems report that they feel the nurturing and help that their support people give them is the most important part of how they cope with motherhood. Money is second. Now, that does not mean that they think money is not important, but rather that the old saying "Money can't buy love" seems to apply here. The feeling of aloneness is better dealt with by having people who care about you and your child than by any number of services and possessions that money can buy.

On the other hand, you cannot responsibly bring a child into the world unless you know that you have sufficient money to support the two of you and provide for your basic needs. You need to have enough for food, housing, and clothing, and also for health care and a car, if you need one. Having a cushion of at least a year's income in savings is recommended, so that you and your child are protected in the event that you lose your job or become seriously ill. Life insurance and other kinds of insurance are usually considered essentials. After these basic expenses and the money you set aside for saving or investing, whatever is left over is discretionary income and can be spent however you prefer.

Two important expenses for which money should be set aside are life insurance, in the event of your death or total disability, and a college fund. Life insurance is one of the most liquid of assets and is paid to your beneficiary within a few weeks of filing the claim. Your other assets may be tied up in any number of complicated ways, but your life insurance will come through. And finally, don't forget to start a college fund early on so that it has time to grow before your child enters college. The time flies faster than you can imagine! There are good financial planners, who can be found through banks, brokerage services, and insurance companies, who specialize in working with people at all income levels, and they can advise you of the relative risks and rewards of various ways of investing.

QUESTIONNAIRE:
IS SINGLE MOTHERHOOD RIGHT FOR YOU?

One of the most important things to do when deciding whether or not you should become an SMC is to allow yourself a thorough process of introspection. With that in mind, here are some questions to help guide you through this self-examination. Only you can answer these questions. They may also spark some other questions. Don't expect to have immediate or perfectly formed answers—give yourself plenty of time to explore your own reactions and responses.

1. Have you accomplished all the personal and career goals that are, in your mind, *essential* to your feeling good about yourself and your life? Can you accept the possibility that you may not achieve some or any of the less essential goals that you still have not reached?

2. Can you hold on to positive feelings about being an SMC while knowing that some people may be critical or disapproving of your decision?

3. Are you in a reasonably secure position to support yourself and a child emotionally and financially?

4. Do you have elderly parents who may need financial and/or practical help? If so, how will their needs be taken care of? Will you be caught between having to take care of a baby and your parent(s)? How will you handle that conflict if it should arise?

5. Have you come to an understanding of why you are not with

a partner at this point in your life? How will that affect your relationship with your child?

6. Are you clear about which of your needs can and will be met by a child and which can only be fulfilled by a mate?

7. How do you cope with stress? Do you have adaptive ways of coping? Assuming that you will be under a great deal of stress during the first year or two of motherhood, can you anticipate that your coping mechanisms will see you through?

8. Can you arrange your life in such a way that you can be assured of a supportive environment for yourself and your child? Does it include a network of support people (friends, relatives, neighbors, etc.) and a support system within your community (church, synagogue, or other house of worship, schools, place of employment, etc.) that you can count on to help you at difficult times?

9. Even though you might have preferred to have a child with a loving partner, can you comfortably acknowledge to yourself, and imagine saying to your son or daughter, that you made a decision and *chose* to become a single mother?

10. Are you prepared for the possibility that the baby of your dreams and fantasies may not be the same baby that you end up with? You have little or no control over such things as the baby's basic temperament and personality. Can you be flexible enough to accept whatever baby you give birth to or adopt?

2

. . . .

BECOMING A SINGLE MOTHER BY
CONCEPTION

There are several ways to become an SMC and only you can decide which way is the best one for you. In this chapter I will discuss becoming pregnant by insemination with donor sperm or by having sex with a man. The following chapter will focus on adoption.

If you find that you are having trouble deciding on how to become pregnant, you may feel better if you realize that this is a very common problem. In my experience talking with "thinkers" during the decision-making period, the decision often seems to be most problematic for those who get caught in the trap of comparing their options as a single woman to the "ideal" or traditional situation. Compared to an ideal situation, any alternative is less ideal, and although as single women we have a number of alternatives, none of them provide the overall societal approval that we might want to have when starting our families. If this is your dilemma, you may have to take a few steps backward and, even if you have already done so, allow yourself to grieve once more for the loss of your dream of bringing a baby into the world with the support of a loving partner. It is painful to grieve, but it also allows you to give up what cannot be and move on to the next step.

The key question is whether or not you can accept the lack of perfection in any of the solutions available to you: a known donor may present legal and/or emotional complications later on, an unknown donor may not give you a very full picture of the biological father. How easy it is to forget that even an apparently good marriage can turn into a nightmare, or that a loving husband can die prematurely. If you really cannot get beyond your feeling that no alternative is good enough, perhaps you need to reinvest your energy and try again to meet a compatible man. But if you can live with the inevitable ambivalence of this kind of compromise, you can then proceed to explore the different possible ways to conceive.

Many women find that keeping a journal or a diary is helpful for sorting out these feelings as part of making such an important decision. Some plan to show their journals to their children when the children are old enough to understand and appreciate the amount of energy and concern that went into their mother's decision to bring them into the world.

THE LEGAL RIGHT OF THE CHILD TO HAVE TWO PARENTS

If you decide to conceive with a man you know, you should keep in mind that in most states he may have the exact same rights as any father *regardless of whether or not you and he were ever married*. The right to support and visitation from both parents is usually viewed by the courts as belonging to the *child*, and you cannot independently decide to keep the father out of your child's life if he wants to be involved, because the law in most states protects the child's right to both parents' involvement. The only exceptions are if you used donor insemination (one reason why this is the preferred method of conception for many women), if the father does not learn that you have borne his child, or if you can prove that the father is dangerous to the child.

CONCEPTION BY DONOR INSEMINATION

For some women the simplest method of becoming an SMC is by donor insemination. Donor insemination (DI for short) has become much more available for single women in recent years as society has become more accepting of single women having babies. There is increased demand from single women—some sperm banks estimate that over 35 percent of their clients are single women—but married couples are also making more use of sperm banks as fertility problems have become more common. You can get inseminated at a sperm bank or at your own gynecologist's or fertility specialist's office, or you can self-inseminate at home. You can use sperm from an unknown donor or from someone you know (referred to as insemination by a known donor).

WHAT IS THE INSEMINATION PROCEDURE?

Insemination is a method of conception whereby a sperm sample is introduced by syringe into a woman's vagina. This procedure can be done with either fresh or frozen sperm, although most doctors are no longer using fresh sperm because of the very serious risk of transmitting AIDS. Although freezing the sperm does not kill the virus, it allows time for the sperm bank to do an HIV blood test on the donor at the point of donation, hold the sperm in a frozen state for six months, and then do a second test on a new sample of the donor's blood. If the second test also comes out negative, it is assumed that the frozen sperm is not carrying the HIV virus and is safe to use.

Insemination is often done two or three times a month around the most fertile time of your cycle, usually immediately before ovulation and again right at the point of ovulation. Simple home ovulation tests, which are sold in drugstores, can enable you to know when you are ovulating, although a doctor may also use ultrasound to look at the egg follicle to be even more certain about the timing, increasing the chances that the insemination is being done at your most fertile time.

Insemination can be done by medical personnel, a friend, or by yourself at home. If done by a medical person, the vagina is opened with a speculum and the sperm is introduced into one of several possible areas of your reproductive tract. Some doctors place the sample higher up than others, believing that more sperm will be able to meet the egg (acid in the vagina kills off millions of sperm). Other doctors place it where it would naturally be with intercourse, believing that the more healthy sperm will be the ones to survive the trip.

If the insemination is done by yourself or a friend at home, the atmosphere is more relaxed and you can stay in bed afterward. (There is some evidence that chances of conception are higher if you do so.)

Intercourse has a higher rate of conception than insemination, possibly because of the hormonal changes that take place along with sexual arousal. Women over thirty-five are at the beginning of a significant decline in their fertility, so many doctors will do a fertility workup if you are over thirty-five and have not become pregnant after three to six months of trying to conceive, regardless of whether you are trying with a sex partner or through insemination. The cost of insemination varies, but about two or three hundred dollars per insemination is average, and most doctors recommend that you be inseminated at least two or possibly three times during your fertile time each cycle. If the insemination is done in a doctor's office, you may get some insurance reimbursement if your policy covers fertility problems, but many do not.

HOW DO YOU FIND RESOURCES FOR DONOR SPERM?

There are several good resources for donor sperm. (Many are listed in Appendix A.) You can go directly to a sperm bank or order sperm from one. You can go to a private fertility doctor who may either have his or her own group of donors or obtain sperm from a sperm bank. With either a doctor or a sperm bank you can usually request at the very least such major characteristics as national origin and religion, but the advantage of large sperm banks is that they usually offer a greater choice of donors and allow you to be more specific about the particular characteristics you might want (coloring, height, talents, hobbies, personality type, etc.). If the sperm bank is affiliated with a hospital, often many of their donors will be medical students and hospital personnel. Once you have conceived with a particular donor, some sperm banks will sell you a supply of extra samples from that same donor. In the event that a mother would like a second child, these samples can be used so that her children will be full siblings.

Some women feel more comfortable using a doctor rather than working with a large sperm bank. However, a doctor may give you less say about your donor, and occasionally we hear of one who chooses the donor entirely at his or her own discretion. You should certainly ask a doctor whom you are considering working with exactly how the donors are selected. Many doctors who inseminate single women will try to match the donor's appearance to the mother's, assuming that this will give the child the best chance of resembling the one parent he or she will be living with—the mother. Whichever source you use, it is important that you thoroughly understand the policies and can accept them.

THE MEDICAL PROFESSION AND SMCS

Members of Single Mothers by Choice across the country have found that in general the medical profession is fairly positive about mature, responsible single women trying to get pregnant by insemination. In some cases, and particularly in more conservative areas of the country, you may find doctors whose personal or religious beliefs make them unwilling to inseminate single women, but in our experience this is not typical of the medical profession as a group. You may want your regular gynecologist to do the inseminations or you might ask for a referral to a fertility specialist. Either way, you need to have sufficiently discussed your decision to become a single mother with the doctor you choose to work with to be sure that you feel respected and supported by him or her.

You should expect the doctor to be at the very least professional about your decision and, ideally, very encouraging. If you live in an area where there are several doctors available to work with, assuming that they are equally competent, you should choose the one with whom you feel the most comfortable. If there is a limited choice of doctors available in your area and you have not been able to find a suitable one, you still have a few options. You can either make the best of working with one who is not your ideal, travel to a good resource in another area, or locate a sperm bank that ships frozen sperm directly to you and do the inseminations yourself.

INSEMINATION WITH SPERM FROM AN UNKNOWN DONOR

SPERM BANKS

Sperm banks are usually profit-making businesses that have facilities for freezing, storing, and selling sperm to women and/or couples who need it. Sometimes they are connected with hospitals, laboratories, or universities, but often they are independent operations, not necessarily run by a medical person. The sperm donors are usually recruited by flyers or by ads in college or local newspapers and are paid for their sperm donation (around fifty dollars per ejaculation is average). The donors tend to be college or graduate students, hospital personnel, or other men who need to make a little extra money to help them with their living expenses. Some sperm banks have strict requirements of the donors such as having a college degree or being married, for example, and others have no particular specifications for donors other than that they be in good health and willing to agree to the sperm bank's rules. Some will specify that a donor will not be allowed to continue to donate sperm after he has fathered a certain number of children, while others have no such limitation. You can and should ask the sperm banks you are considering to tell you what criteria they use in selecting donors.

A small but increasing minority of sperm banks will ask the donor to designate whether or not he is willing to permit the children he has fathered to contact him when they are over eighteen (sometimes these donors are referred to as "yes" donors). If the donor agrees to this, it is the child's option to do so or not. This last criterion is very important to many SMCs because, while they would like the child to have the option of finding out who the father is later on, they still want to feel secure that the donor will not be able to locate them. I recommend that you have a lawyer review your contract with the sperm bank, as well as the donor's, to be sure that your anonymity is securely protected.

Sperm banks change their guidelines all the time, so when you contact them, ask them to send you literature on their current policies, including what percentage, if any, of their donors are "yes" donors. Don't be shy about asking for specific and detailed information, and beware of a sperm bank that gives you vague answers or platitudes such as "All our donors are excellent."

Some good questions to ask are: How do they define excellent? What, if any, requirements do they have of their donors? How many donors are there for you to select from? How much and what sort of information are you allowed to know about the potential donors before you choose one? How many children are the donors permitted to father? What kind of medical information about the donor is available to you after you become a mother? What percentage of each ejaculate is given to the recipient?

Often the donors are asked to abstain from sex for at least two days prior to donating sperm in order to make their ejaculation as large as possible. The sperm sample given to you is a portion of an ejaculation, not the whole amount. Most banks will divide an ejaculation into many parts so as to maximize their profits. As an informed consumer, you might want to compare sperm banks to see which ones give larger samples. Some may divide it into as many as ten portions, while others divide it only into thirds. All the banks claim that they give more than ample sperm for a woman to conceive with, but more sperm can only help your chances of conception. The sperm bank should test each donation for motility and sperm count and also for venereal disease.

Since most sperm banks are using only frozen sperm today, and it can easily be shipped, you have a wide choice of sperm banks from anywhere in the country, so be a smart shopper. If your doctor has his or her own source of sperm donors, ask the same questions. If you are not satisfied with the answers, ask if you can get sperm from another source and bring it in to the doctor's office. Alternatively, you might want to consider self-insemination at home.

All sperm banks should, at the very minimum, require their donors to fill out a family health history and submit to a blood test for AIDS. As described earlier, if the blood test comes back negative, the frozen sperm donation is kept until six months later, at which point the donor is given another blood test. If the second AIDS test comes back negative, then the sperm is used.

There have been some problems with sperm banks in recent years, as you may have seen in the media. Dr. Cecil Jacobson, a doctor who ran a sperm bank in Virginia, is now in prison after he was found to have used his own sperm to inseminate his patients. He may have fathered as many as seventy-five children. Another publicized case was that of a New York sperm bank that gave a woman sperm which was supposedly from her husband, but which turned out to be from another person entirely. It was a substitution that might never have been discovered except that the woman's husband was white and the baby was black. The sperm bank was able to trace the sperm sample back to a black sperm donor and it turned out that it had been a simple case of human error in mislabeling sperm samples, but one that had enormous emotional, moral, and legal implications. While you cannot expect your sperm bank to be perfect, don't be afraid to ask them about what precautions they take to assure that you are getting the sperm you requested.

The most common reason SMCs give for choosing insemination with an unknown donor is that it is the simplest method of conception available to them. There are virtually no legal complications, present or future, because the policies of most sperm banks make it nearly impossible to learn the identities of the donors (except in the case of a "yes" donor, as explained above). Therefore you do not have to worry about the biological father locating the child and contesting custody or wanting visitation, nor does the donor have to worry about any financial responsibility for the child. Again, you may want an attorney to review both your contract and the donor's to assure that you are as protected as possible.

How Much Information Can You Have About the Donor?
The amount of information about the donor given to you varies greatly depending upon the policies of the sperm bank that you (or your doctor) choose. They may not tell you much about the donor except some basic facts such as his ethnic and religious background, educational level, and possibly some physical characteristics such as height and hair and eye color. The more progressive sperm banks or doctors will give you additional information about the donor such as his interests

and talents. Some may show you a profile written by the donor describing himself and his reasons for becoming a sperm donor, and some will give you a photo or videotape.

One SMC described the process of picking a sperm donor as "a bizarre sort of blind date" and many SMCs have mentioned that they felt a kind of crush on or love for their donor after having been inseminated or after having conceived his child. In some cases the women get a crush on the doctor doing the insemination and occasionally they develop a fantasy that it was his sperm and therefore it is his baby that they are carrying, rather than that of an unknown donor. I do not think of this as some temporary form of insanity, but more that it reflects a natural desire to feel some real and positive connection with the man who is the biological father of your child. We can all understand that this is a more comfortable and reassuring thought than the fact that we are going to be conceiving with a total stranger.

If it is important to you that your child be able to locate his father when he is an adult, you should choose one of the sperm banks that permit the donors to specify if they would be willing to be contacted by their offspring ("yes" donors). These sperm banks say that about half of their donors choose that option.

Confidentiality of Sperm Bank Records

There is some controversy regarding the confidentiality of sperm banks' records that is due in part to the differing needs of infertile couples and of single women seeking a sperm donor. Infertile couples frequently feel very strongly that the utmost confidentiality should be maintained, in large part because of the shame connected with infertility. Although many experts disagree with this advice, couples are often advised by the sperm bank personnel not to tell their child that her "dad" is not her biological father for fear that this information might create a barrier between the child and the dad. However, there is considerable research and clinical evidence in the area of child development that indicates that secrecy in the family, especially about such a major issue as a family member's origins, causes more problems than it solves. A book called *Lethal Secrets*, by Annette Baran and Reuben Pannor, which includes interviews with sperm donors, parents who used donor sperm, and children born of insemination, makes a strong case for the viewpoint that secrecy in families is harmful and appeals for a more open policy in this area.

After years of studying children who were adopted, we have learned that the secrecy that was maintained in the past was frequently troubling and damaging to all the parties involved and that the children often felt betrayed when they eventually learned the truth. They felt that because it had been kept a secret there was something wrong or shameful about having been adopted. It is possible that policies regarding the anonymity of donor insemination will follow the trend of adoption regulations, which have gradually shifted from being very strict and secretive toward greater openness about the identities of the parties involved. I believe this would be best for all concerned.

A single woman, unlike some married couples, might very much want her child to have access to the records at age eighteen so that he could have the opportunity to find out as much as possible about his biological father and maybe even meet him. There might be some fears about the donor also having access to the records and trying to become involved in the child's life, but realistically, many donors father a number of children and the likelihood of a donor deciding to get involved is not very great. The donor, we should add, also might have fears of future financial liability should the mother decide to contest the legality of his surrendering his paternal rights and responsibilities.

IMPLICATIONS FOR THE CHILD OF DONOR INSEMINATION

If you conceive with donor insemination you need to be aware of some of the emotional implications for your child. Because you have so little information about the donor, when your child starts asking questions about her father (usually at around age three) you will have to help her come to terms with the fact that you don't know and may never know much about the biological father. You may not be able to share photos or anecdotes about him, just some facts about a few characteristics. If you haven't worked out how you feel about this lack of information, you may be uncomfortable about it and feel guilty when your child pressures you for facts that you do not have.

Laurie

One night at eleven-thirty I got a call from Laurie, an SMC whose daughter, Ellen, age nine, had been conceived by donor insemination. Laurie had just gotten Ellen to sleep after a night of tearful discussion about the fact that they knew almost nothing about Ellen's father. According to Laurie, Ellen had always been at ease with the situation and, in fact, had been able to talk about it in what seemed like a genuinely comfortable way. Laurie told me how Ellen had suddenly come to her and burst into tears, saying, ''I love you, Mom, you know I do, but I'm really mad that you don't know much about my father. Some of the other SMC kids have seen pictures of their fathers, some know their names, and I know *nothing*! How could you do this to me?" Laurie told me she hugged Ellen and cried with her for a bit and finally said to her, "You know, Ellen, I feel sad about it too. I wish I could have known more and could tell you more about him. But that wasn't possible and I wanted you so badly that I decided to have you even if I couldn't do it in the most perfect way."

Ellen's unexpected outburst had stirred up Laurie's residual feelings of guilt about her decision to conceive with DI. Very upset and concerned for Ellen, Laurie asked me what she had done wrong. I responded that I didn't think she had done anything wrong, and that in fact this was a very important and necessary phase for Ellen to go through. We sometimes forget that our children are not alone in having conflicts and confused feelings about their lives and upbringings that they have to work out. This is true of all children.

As I told Laurie, it seemed to me quite understandable and natural that Ellen, who for the most part had felt fine about the facts of her conception, at times would also be upset, angry, or confused about it. I was especially impressed by the fact that Laurie hadn't rushed in to tell Ellen that she shouldn't feel sad, and, in fact, had validated Ellen's feelings and told her that she even shared them at times. This is a lovely example of a mother who can permit her child to experience and express her anger and confusion, and respond to it with empathy rather than defensiveness or denial. By so doing, she keeps open the channels of communication with her child.

Another important consideration when you choose to conceive by DI is what *your* feelings are about having conceived in this nontraditional way. How would you feel in the situation described above if you were Laurie? In order to do the best possible job of explaining these issues to your child, you yourself have to be comfortable with having made the choice to conceive with an unknown donor. I'll include much more about the children's feelings and how to handle them in Chapter 5, where I discuss how to tell your child about his or her father.

ADVANTAGES TO CONCEIVING WITH AN UNKNOWN DONOR

Debbie

Conceiving with an unknown donor was essential to Debbie, a thirty-two-year-old travel agent. She was very much concerned and afraid that a known donor might change his mind and decide that he wanted to have frequent contact with his child and maybe even sue for custody. She imagined a worst-case scenario that involved the donor getting married and trying to conceive a child with his wife, only to learn that his wife was infertile. Then, she felt sure, he would decide to fight for custody of the child he had conceived with Debbie, and since he was married and she was single, the court might feel it was in the best interest of the child for him to live with two parents.

Debbie had been raised in a family that was shattered by a bitter divorce and custody battle when she was a small child, and she was determined that she would never put any child of hers through such a devastating experience, nor did she ever want to have to go through anything similar herself. From her point of view, whatever qualms she might have about insemination with sperm from an unknown donor, and whatever complications there might be down the road in explaining things to her child, they were well worth it in order to guarantee her custody of her future child.

Debbie went to a few fertility specialists until she found one who she felt was both competent and very reassuring that the donor's identity would never be known. She went through about six inseminations, and after blood tests revealed that she had a slight hormonal deficiency, she was given some medication and then conceived on her eighth attempt. She is now the proud mother of a healthy baby girl and is considering having a second child.

Given Debbie's background and family history, it is understandable that she felt so strongly that she had to minimize the risk of any kind of future family disruption. She chose what felt to her like the best route to assure her peace of mind and security as she started a family of her own.

INSEMINATION WITH SPERM FROM A KNOWN DONOR

It may be important to you to know the biological father of your child and to be able to tell your child about him from firsthand experience rather than from facts given to you by a third party. In that case, you may prefer to conceive with sperm from someone you know. If so, you need to decide whether you want to conceive by insemination or by having sex with him.

Whichever way you decide to proceed, be *sure* to have the man agree to a blood test for HIV and be fully aware of the risk you are taking. *Even if the test is negative, there is no guarantee that he has not contracted the HIV virus and is not carrying it, since it apparently takes about six months after it is contracted to be detect-*

able by a blood test. You may want to do what the sperm banks do: freeze his sperm donations and not use them until he has been retested six months later and still tests negative. Or, at the very least, have him tested when he agrees to be your donor and again every six months until after you conceive, just to give yourself the peace of mind of knowing that he wasn't carrying the virus while you were using his sperm.

Sex or Insemination?

Some women feel that conception without sex is just too impersonal and are uncomfortable about separating conception from the sex act. Others feel that conceiving by insemination is preferable because there is less possibility of an emotional involvement with the man. Insemination also indicates to the world that you clearly *chose* from the beginning to become a single mother. Some SMCs feel strongly that they do not want there to be any reason for people to think that their pregnancy was accidental.

If you decide that you want to be inseminated with sperm from a known donor, you may have many choices of donors available to you or you may have great difficulty in finding anyone who is willing to help you conceive. It partially depends upon how much effort and creativity you are willing to put into your search for a potential donor and is also to some degree a matter of luck.

Some women are very determined to use a known donor and persist in seeking out the right person through every possible avenue. They tell everyone they know, they advertise, they make it a priority in how they spend their time and energy. When they find a possible donor, they spend a great deal of time getting to know the person and clarifying what his expectations, needs, and wishes concerning parenthood might be and letting him know about theirs. They discuss the various possible degrees of his involvement with the future child, ranging from no participation to coparenting, they try to determine whether they share similar expectations, and ultimately they draw up an agreement or a statement of intentions. (See Appendix C for examples of such an agreement.)

If the man wants to be a coparent, is it likely to work? Do the two of you know each other's values, and are they similar? What about educational philosophies and child-rearing beliefs? On the other hand, if the man is not interested in any involvement, why is he volunteering to father a child and how clear is he about the implications? Might he change his mind? What if he does change his mind? You have to be prepared for the fact that by using a known donor, you are potentially surrendering your right to raise your child alone.

Some SMCs have adapted the scenario of *The Big Chill*, a popular movie from 1983 in which a single woman has sex with the husband of a close friend who already has children of her own. In the film the man volunteers to help her conceive as a gift to her because she is someone whom both he and his wife care about very much. In real life the complications in this kind of situation are fairly apparent—sex with a friend's husband can ignite jealousy and/or passion despite the belief of all parties that they are too mature and civilized for something like that to happen. Then there is the issue of what to tell the child and ultimately the community about the child's paternity. This is less complicated if the families do not live near one another, but if they are in the same town it can create a lot of problems once the child starts telling people about her father.

If you want to find a donor yourself, look at it as a challenge or as a quest for something essential—you will need to use your creativity, your judgment, and your networking skills to their maximum capacity. With that approach, most women who want to find an appropriate donor are able to do so.

SOME SERIOUS CONSIDERATIONS IF CONCEIVING WITH A KNOWN DONOR

When you decide to conceive with someone you know, you must be clear that there are potential *major* legal and emotional complications that will continue throughout your child's life. *The biological father's legal rights in most states are exactly the same whether you and he were ever married or not,* so by conceiving a child with a man you know, you are opening the door to having some involvement with him at some point or even ongoing involvement. He may decide he wants to have visitation or joint custody, he may be able to prevent you from moving out of the area or from taking the child out of the country, and he may challenge your decisions. In short, you may end up coparenting to some degree if or whenever he chooses to become involved. You would, of course, be entitled to child support.

On the other hand, you and he may be able to develop a good working partnership as coparents. This is not easy to do, but if it works it can be a real plus because you will be giving your child many of the benefits of having two parents, as in what we sometimes refer to as a "good divorce," but without the prior devastation and disruption that comes with a divorce. Of course he may not choose to become involved at all, in which case you have total autonomy.

Marilyn

After thinking about it for nearly two years, Marilyn, a business-woman, age thirty-three, realized that conceiving with sperm from an unknown donor was not the right choice for her. She felt she had to know the biological father of her child, at least to some minimal degree. Marilyn decided to try to find a man who was willing to donate fresh sperm to help her conceive. She started to search for such a person at age thirty-three primarily because she thought she might want to have two children, and because she wanted to be a mother while she still had a great deal of energy and physical stamina. She was concurrently dating and looking for a potential spouse, but she made it clear to the men she was seeing that she was intending to start a family in the very near future as a single mother.

She spoke to everyone she knew and told them she was interested in finding a healthy man to be a sperm donor. She even put an ad in the local newspaper under the heading of "Medical Services Needed." Several of her friends helped her find men who were willing to discuss the possibility of being donors, and seven men, all of them very serious about it, responded to her ad.

Marilyn met or spoke with all of them and narrowed the selection down to four who had the kinds of characteristics that were important to her. She then sat down with each of them individually and talked about the kinds of relationships they wanted to have with the future child. Some wanted no contact at all and some wanted considerable involvement, so Marilyn realized that she had to clarify what kind of future relationship *she* felt comfortable with. She decided that what she wanted was minimal or no contact with the man, at least until the child turned eighteen.

She then told each of the potential donors who met her criteria that she would expect them not to request visitation or custody and that she would not request any child support. She particularly favored two of the men, partly because of the kind of people they were and partly because they were both planning in the near future to leave the Chicago area, where Marilyn lived. They were both willing to help Marilyn conceive a child for the same reason: they were not sure that they were ever going to marry and yet they wanted to know that they would have a child on the earth, without any of the entanglements of a family. She decided to pursue the exploration further with these two.

Marilyn was worried about the possible transmission of the HIV virus so she asked each of the two potential donors to go for an HIV test. They both tested negative and agreed that they would go for a second test in six months, which would assure (at least as far as medical science today can assure) that they had not contracted the HIV virus prior to its being detectable by a blood test. Meanwhile they donated sperm, which was frozen and held in storage at a sperm bank. Marilyn paid for all expenses involved in the testing and storage of the frozen sperm.

The next step was to draw up a document that made it clear that Marilyn was intending to conceive a child with a known donor and that she would not ask for or expect any financial support from that donor. It also clarified that the donor understood that he was not going to be taking part in the child's life in any way until after the child was legally an adult according to the laws of Illinois, the state where Marilyn lived—and then only if the contact was mutually agreeable. (Two examples of an agreement between an SMC and a known donor can be found in Appendix C.)

Marilyn then gave both men a copy of the written agreement to read. Each took it to a lawyer who explained (as had Marilyn) that the document may or may not be legally binding and that if either the donor or Marilyn were to change their minds about any part of it and challenge it in court, it might be of no legal value. (As explained above, a child has a legal right to support from and visitation with both its biological parents unless otherwise specified by a court and no parent can take away this right, or the father's parental rights, by any sort of agreement or contract, written or otherwise.) On the other hand, the lawyers agreed, if neither Marilyn nor the donor wanted to alter it, the agreement was excellent as a statement of intentions and as a clarification of the situation for the parties involved.

Both men were willing to go along with the agreement and felt they could trust Marilyn to keep her end of it. (She had a successful business of her own and a secure financial situation, so the likelihood that she would need financial support was remote.) Both of the men were willing to be contacted when the child was eighteen. After waiting six months for the follow-up blood tests, Marilyn then proceeded to be inseminated with the sperm that had been frozen, alternating donors each month so that she would know which one was the father. She conceived in the fourth month of trying and now has a healthy baby boy.

CONCEPTION WITH A SEX PARTNER

Some SMCs conceive with a sex partner by accident, others have planned pregnancies with a cooperative partner, and some have planned pregnancies with an unsuspecting partner. Unless the man knowingly helped you conceive, you will have to decide whether or not to tell him about the pregnancy. You should consider this issue from both moral and legal points of view before reaching a decision.

As to the reasons behind choosing this method, one woman I spoke with in a recent workshop told me that when people ask why she did not choose to use donor insemination for her (planned) pregnancy she replied, "Well, I guess I'm just too traditional." Some women just do not feel comfortable using an anonymous donor or with the insemination process itself and prefer to conceive in a way that is closer to the traditional.

ACCIDENTAL CONCEPTION

You might accidentally have become pregnant with a lover (yes, a woman in her mid-thirties who is familiar with birth control does sometimes accidentally get pregnant). There is always the possibility of human error when using birth control, or perhaps you were less careful than usual, thinking that you were unlikely to conceive at your age. On the other hand, you might have wanted to conceive but were not able to admit it to yourself.

If you conceived accidentally it is important that you take note of your initial or gut reaction when you first learned you were pregnant. This response is a good indication of whether or not you're emotionally ready to seriously consider going ahead with the pregnancy and becoming an SMC. Perhaps you were surprised to find yourself pleased rather than horrified. Or maybe you thought you would have been happy with the news, but in fact felt terrible. You then need to evaluate these feelings and try to clarify why you felt them.

With an accidental conception, it is crucial to come to terms with your relationship with the biological father and with your own sense of whether your priority is continuing the relationship with the man or fulfilling your desire to become a mother. You also need to take into account the feelings of the other person. Your partner may be very clear about not wanting to become a parent, or he may be confused and need to sort out his feelings.

A man who had unknowingly impregnated a woman he was dating wrote an interesting article for *Mothering* magazine in which he presented a man's perspective on single motherhood by choice.* When she told him of her pregnancy, the woman assured him that he did not need to be involved. After initially being angry at her for having "stolen" his sperm, he was then relieved at being "let off the hook" and made plans to move far away before she changed her mind. Later, after having moved over a thousand miles away, he found himself having different feelings. He realized that he had initially reacted out of fear and had seen the situation only as posing a potential financial burden. However, with the passage of time, he came to the conclusion that by avoiding his responsibilities as a father he might also be missing out on an opportunity to have some very positive experiences. He decided to reestablish contact with his child's mother and let her know that he would be sending child support payments, and also that he would like to have some visits with his child from time to time. He and his child got to know one another slowly. The visits were initially in the mother's home, but when the child was old enough he began to visit his father. The author ended his article by recommending to other men in his situation that they not be afraid of the responsibilities of fatherhood and that they instead look at the opportunities it presents to them. This is certainly one scenario that an SMC might find workable if she and the father can stay on reasonably cordial or even friendly terms.

Both you and the man involved may well have a series of

*McFarland, Thom R. "Disposable Daddies." *Mothering*, Fall 1991, pp. 116–19.

reactions to becoming a parent—perhaps terrified initially but then more and more positive about it or, alternatively, less and less enthusiastic after at first being pleased. You and your lover will do best if you can be respectful of one another's need to have different feelings at different times and give one another time and space to come to terms with this unexpected pregnancy. It would also be helpful if the two of you could get some short-term couple counseling to help you sort out the very complex issues. I know from the many different experiences of our SMC group members and from my work with the many couples I have counseled how difficult and upsetting this decision-making process can be for both partners.

Carolyn

Carolyn, a thirty-four-year-old teacher, had been thinking about becoming a single mother but was unsure if she was comfortable with the idea of having a child without being married. She decided she would experiment with the idea and not use birth control the next time she had sex in order to see how she felt about conceiving this way. It fleetingly crossed her mind that she might actually become pregnant during this "experiment" but she felt it was highly unlikely. Her mother had tried for over a year before conceiving her, and at a much younger age, and most of Carolyn's married friends around her age had had difficulty becoming pregnant.

A former lover who now lived in a different city was planning to visit Carolyn during a phase in her cycle when she was fairly sure she would not be ovulating, and she decided that if they made love she would forgo the birth control just this one time. They did make love one night during his visit, and when she awoke the next morning she thought, "What if I had gotten pregnant? I couldn't do that without telling him. It doesn't feel right." She decided that her experiment had shown her that this was not the way for her to become a mother, and she decided she would not do it again.

A few weeks later Carolyn had terrible indigestion and her period was late. Friends suggested that she might be pregnant, but Carolyn insisted that was impossible. The one time she had sex when she had not used birth control was during a time in her cycle when she thought she could not possibly have been ovulating. When her period didn't come after seven weeks and she was so bloated that she thought she would burst, she decided to take a pregnancy test. Much to her amazement, she was pregnant—and she was thrilled. She realized immediately that she wanted this baby, and she felt truly lucky to have been able to conceive so easily, almost literally without even trying.

The decision about what to tell her former boyfriend was not so easy. Carolyn thought at first about not telling him at all. She was pretty sure that he would not be happy about it, and perhaps he would even be angry at her. She also wanted to spare him whatever emotional stress she could. Since any serious relationship was clearly over and they rarely saw one another anymore, it was possible that he might never find out about the pregnancy. But on the other hand, she also wanted to be fair and give him the opportunity to be involved if he wanted to be. She didn't want her child to feel later on that she had prevented the father from participating in their lives.

Carolyn decided to tell him. He was shocked at first to learn that she was intending to have the baby and worried that she would ask him for financial help. He made it clear that he did not want to be involved in any way. Carolyn assured him that she was willing and able to take on the responsibility by herself and that she would not be expecting or asking for any financial help from him. She also told him that if he ever changed his mind and wanted to participate, he would be welcome in their lives. Carolyn gave birth to a healthy baby girl and has always felt very grateful for this man's unwitting contribution to her happiness.

Carolyn's accidental pregnancy is an example of what sometimes happens when a woman can't allow herself to fully acknowledge her desire to become pregnant or take complete responsibility for choosing to become pregnant, but finds it easier to make the choice after the fact, once the pregnancy is a reality.

IF YOU ARE DEEPLY INVOLVED WITH THE FATHER

The primary issue in an accidental conception is your relationship with the biological father. Is he someone you have a serious and caring relationship with? If so, you and he have some difficult soul-searching to do about how each of you feels about parenthood. In one possible scenario you may both agree that the pregnancy is a blessed event and you and he will be able to work out how much of an involvement he will have with the baby. All levels of his participation are possible, from none to minimal to marriage.

If you and he decide that he will be involved as an active parent, I strongly recommend that together you draw up a written agreement for the purpose of clarifying exactly how you each see your roles and responsibilities with regard to your future child. This is important in order to be sure that you both share the same intentions, and the more you can spell out the details, the better. A general statement such as "We agreed to coparent the child" is a beginning, but you will need to spell out what that means in terms of finances (including living expenses, but also such things as medical, tuition, and camp expenses, and eventually inheritance), whether or not the father's name appears on the birth certificate, decision-making responsibilities, and other important issues. (See Appendix C for two sample agreements.) In the process of drawing up such a document you will get to know more about one another's points of view concerning children and have a chance to discover how you work together on a joint venture. This can be enlightening in terms of how you will work together as coparents. You should have a lawyer review your agreement to be sure that all relevant legal issues are considered.

If you end up coparenting with someone, you are not, strictly speaking, a single mother. Although you may face some of the same issues as an SMC, most of your struggles and concerns will be more typical of someone who is married or divorced.

On the other hand, if the two of you disagree about whether or not to have the baby, you ultimately will each have to sort out which is more important to you, the relationship or the baby. It may be similar to that awful question about being in a boat that is sinking with two people you love on board and only being able to save one of them. How does one make this kind of decision?

If you were hoping that the news about the accidental pregnancy would improve your relationship, perhaps bringing a greater degree of commitment from the man, you could be in for a big disappointment. Few of us respond at our best to an ultimatum or to having to make a major decision under duress. If you insist on a commitment, you may actually alienate your lover and make him distrustful of you. At best he will probably feel very torn and conflicted. As mentioned earlier, couple counseling can be very helpful in sorting out the issues and clarifying your feelings since neither one of you can be expected to be entirely objective at a time like this.

If you can allow yourself to examine your feelings about the accidental pregnancy without jumping to any conclusions, you may find yourself evaluating the relationship in a different way now that there is the possibility of bearing this man's child. Is he someone whom you feel would be a good father? Do you want him more involved in your life (as he will be if you have his child)? On the other hand, you may find yourself getting excited about being a mother while feeling less desire to be with your partner than you had previously. Or you may be dismayed about the pregnancy and be very clear that the relationship is your priority right now. Your age may be a factor here. A woman in her early thirties may feel that there is a good chance for another pregnancy in a few years, with this man or another, whereas a woman in her late thirties may feel this is her last chance to have her biological child.

It may be important also to look at your feelings about bearing and raising this particular man's child. How do you feel about him? Can you imagine what it would be like for you if the child turns out to be like him or to physically resemble him? What if your partner is very clear that he does not want to be a parent? Or if he does, what kind of influence will he be on a child? How stable and mature is he?

If you tell the father and he feels strongly that he does not want to be a parent, that simplifies your decision. As one SMC said to me recently, "The minute I heard his response to the news that I was pregnant I knew that it was over between us. I couldn't be with a man who was able to just walk away from his child like that."

It is a terrible choice to have to make. If you and your lover end up separating because he didn't want to be involved and you decided that having the baby was more important to you than the relationship, you will be in essentially the same position as a divorced mother. You will be angry and grieving about losing someone you love and all your fantasies of a future together, while at the same time having to emotionally prepare yourself for the new role of single mother.

IMPLICATIONS FOR THE CHILD

The degree of involvement you had with the father is a crucial matter that carries lasting implications for your relationship with your child. If you were deeply involved with the man and hoped that the relationship was going to lead to a serious commitment, you have to accept the fact that this child will forever link you to that person. It can be bittersweet—you will inevitably see aspects of your ex-lover in the child, and many memories will be stirred up as you answer your child's questions and tell him about his father. On the other hand, *if* you can keep your anger and disappointment in perspective and forgive him for his failings and limitations (and this is a crucial "if"), the fact that you once loved this man can be a real help to your child as he begins to try to come to terms with his origins. If you are able to convey the loving feelings you once had for the father when talking about him, and if your child sees a loving light in your eyes as you discuss him, it will help your child to have positive feelings toward him, which in turn will help her, if a daughter, develop positive feelings toward men in general, and will help him, if a son, feel good about his male identity, which is inexorably linked to his father. If it is not possible for there to be a loving light in your eyes, you owe it to your child to come up with at least a neutral attitude. If you can't get there on your own, go for some counseling to resolve your feelings while your child is still too young to be asking about his father.

If the father is someone with whom you have had a relatively casual relationship, you may be in a situation that one of our SMC members described as having had "insemination with a sex partner," meaning that you and the father were temporarily involved but you were clear that this relationship had no potential for a commitment. Perhaps you even thought, deep in the recesses of your mind, that this might be a good person with whom to get pregnant and were less than meticulous about birth control. You may have already lost contact with the man or may decide to end your casual relationship without telling him of the pregnancy, or you may decide to tell him and work out some agreement about his participation in the child's life, drawing up an agreement as described above. You will at some point have to tell your child about this man—she will want to know what he was like and whether she has anything in common with him, and so you will need to come up with whatever positives you can find, even if the man was not someone with whom you were particularly close. Keep in mind that your child will forever link you to a man who will have more importance to her (as her biological father) than he ever had to you as a brief or casual lover.

IF YOU ARE NOT DEEPLY INVOLVED
WITH THE FATHER

On the other hand, if you are not very involved emotionally with the father, your situation may be somewhat easier. In this case, the degree of difficulty you have with the decision will depend primarily upon how sure you feel about being ready to become a single mother and how clear each of you is about what kind of involvement, if any, the father wants to have.

If you both see it the same way, fine. If you have different ideas about what the future relationships will be with one another and with the child, then you need to do your best to sort it all out and come to a decision that is workable for both of you. Will you continue to be lovers and will he also play a role in the child's life? Or will he have some degree of involvement with the child but not with you? Would you want to continue to see him if he is not interested in the child? How will you feel if he is interested only in the child?

Whatever you decide, it is helpful for the two of you to consult a lawyer in order to draw up some kind of a written agreement that clearly states what responsibilities each of you agrees to take on as a parent and also what each of you expects of the other. (See Appendix C for two examples of such an agreement.) While this document takes away rights that legally belong to the child and the father, and so probably won't hold up in court should either of you change your mind and want to challenge its legality, it is nonetheless helpful to go through the process of clarification with one another in order to minimize confusion and unstated expectations. And couple counseling can be helpful, not only to sort out feelings about one another, but also to clarify what kinds of feelings each of you has about the child.

Please remember: In this age of sexually transmitted diseases it is very, *very* risky to have unprotected sex. If you are able to have the father take a blood test for HIV, do so, and if not, have yourself and the baby tested just to make sure that you have nothing to worry about.

And once again, remember that if you have a child with someone you know, he has the same rights and responsibilities as if you were married, and you are entitled to child support from him if you request it.

TO TELL OR NOT TO TELL THE FATHER

If you have become pregnant by accident and are delighted and decide to go ahead with the pregnancy, you will probably do fine as an SMC. However, you will need to decide whether or not to tell the father that you are pregnant and having his child. Some women, like Carolyn, who conceived with a former lover, feel that they want to be fair to everyone concerned and give the man the opportunity to decide what kind of involvement, if any, he wants. They also feel it is important that when the child someday asks if his father knew about him, they can say that he did, and that the decision not to be involved was his. They hope that this will reassure their child that they did not want to keep the father away or prevent his involvement in any way.

IF THE FATHER IS UNSTABLE OR ABUSIVE

This can be complicated in a situation where the father is a person whom you do not feel comfortable involving in your future because he is unstable or would be a bad influence on a child. In such instances it might be best not to tell the man if you believe it would present an unresolvable or potentially dangerous situation. If he is someone whose whereabouts you can keep track of, you have the option of telling him at a later point if and when the child may want to know him. Alternatively, you may not be able to locate the man in the future and will have to help your child understand that it is not always possible to find someone, and that you had good reasons for not wanting to stay in touch with his father.

If you are quite clear that the risks of continued exposure

to the father outweigh the positives, and if you feel you cannot handle the implications of any future involvement with him, consider whether or not you can manage for him never to find out. If not, you need to decide whether you can live with the risk of his future participation in your life, or whether the options of either terminating the pregnancy or giving the child up for adoption make sense to you (particularly if you are still in your early thirties or younger). A number of women I have spoken to at SMC meetings have told me that they had previously ended a pregnancy because the relationship with the potential father promised to be terribly complicated and they felt it was not the way they wanted to embark upon motherhood. Their accidental pregnancies had helped them realize that they wanted to become mothers, but this time they were planning to conceive by donor insemination. Other women feel that they cannot in good conscience abort a life simply because the circumstances are too knotty, and decide to go ahead and have the baby with the full understanding that they and the child will be living with a situation that will be extremely demanding and complex.

Shari

Shari, a teacher, became pregnant accidentally at age thirty-six with a man she had known for quite a while. She knew she would never marry him as she did not feel he was reliable or mature enough, and he had also made it clear that he was not ready for marriage. Nevertheless, she continued to see him because he was fun to be with and a good social and sexual companion.

When Shari realized she was pregnant and told him that she intended to have the child as a single mother, he was furious. He wanted her to marry him and when she refused he told her he wanted her to have an abortion. Shari said that she was sorry that he felt that way, but that she had no intentions of either marrying him or of having an abortion. She wanted to be a single mother, she told him. In an attempt to dissuade her from having the baby alone, he threatened to sue for visitation or custody, but Shari remained sure that she wanted to become a single mother. She told him he was welcome to visit the baby, but that was the extent of the involvement she was willing to have with him.

Shari hoped that he would eventually realize that she meant what she said and would calm down. After she gave birth she was worried about even letting him visit the baby because his behavior was so irrational and threatening. Nevertheless, she did allow him to visit and spend time with their son after he was born.

The visits were very unpleasant. He kept badgering Shari to marry him, constantly shouted at her, accusing her of being selfish and manipulative, and threatened to make her life miserable until she agreed to his terms. Shari told him that he had to pull himself together and behave appropriately in front of the baby or she would not allow him to visit at all, but this threat just made him angrier. Ultimately he took Shari to court, claiming that she was an inadequate mother, and they had a year-long battle over custody. The court eventually ruled in Shari's favor and limited him to supervised visits until he could control himself better. Although Shari won a legal victory, she spent several thousand dollars on legal fees and paid a great emotional price as well. She anticipates continuing struggles with this man, and says that if it weren't for the fact that she loves the child so much, she would say that she regrets ever having had his baby.

As this example illustrates, it is important to realize that your decisions about whether or not to tell and *how* you tell the father about your pregnancy have lifelong consequences for you, for the father, and for your child. If you decide not to tell the father, that also has long-term consequences, because your child may well ask you whether or not her father knew about her birth and if not, why not. Remember also that if the father suspects it is his child, he can get a court order to compel the child to have an HLA test, which is a genetic screening (done from a blood sample) that establishes paternity. It is a matter you should think through very carefully.

FERTILITY PROBLEMS AND INFERTILITY

Many single women put off thinking about whether or not they want to be mothers for a long time—sometimes for too long. Fertility in women declines markedly after age thirty-five and dramatically after forty, yet in this era of amazing reproductive technology some women feel they don't have to worry about making this big decision until their forties and then, having finally decided to go ahead and have a baby, they find themselves faced with frustrating and expensive fertility problems.

You may be able to find a good fertility specialist who will work with single women (see the section on the medical profession and single mothers, page 29) and, if you are lucky, you will be one of the ones who has a treatable problem. Sometimes, however, the problem is of unknown origin, and you will have to decide how much is enough when it comes to trying different methods to solve the problems. Drugs such as Clomid and Pergonal are often used to regulate and stimulate egg production (sometimes resulting in multiple births). Women report that going through the regimen of fertility tests, drugs, hormone injections, and other sometimes risky or even medically unsanctioned treatments month after month can be an emotionally draining and sometimes devastating experience, besides being very expensive. You will need to determine how long you are willing and able (emotionally and financially) to go through these procedures.

Sometimes the process can become an obsession that is in the forefront of your mind nearly all the time. First there are the days of waiting for the signs of ovulation, then there is the insemination, which you hope will work this time, and then there is the hopeful phase of feeling sure that it has worked—and then you learn that it hasn't.

Many SMCs say that when they go through these monthly cycles they feel they are on an emotional roller coaster unlike anything they have experienced before. At some point you have to decide whether you are able to change direction and start trying to adopt or whether you cannot take that step and would prefer to forgo motherhood altogether.

There is a national organization called RESOLVE, which helps people who have fertility problems, and they can give you the most current information on fertility treatments and also refer you to a local support group to help you make this most difficult decision. If it turns out that you are infertile, the group also will support you as you go through the necessary grieving for the biological child you never will have. RE-SOLVE has local chapters in most cities, and they do include single women in their groups, although their membership consists predominantly of infertile couples. Some of the larger local chapters of Single Mothers by Choice also have groups for single women who have been trying to conceive for over a year without success that address similar issues as do the RESOLVE groups.

3

BECOMING A SINGLE MOTHER
BY ADOPTION

The world of adoption is an extremely complex one, in part because there are so many variables. You will need to make some important decisions: whether to go the route of agencies, public or private, or pursue an independent adoption on your own or with the help of an intermediary such as an adoption lawyer; whether you want an open or a closed adoption; whether you prefer a baby or a toddler or an older child; whether you have a preference for a boy or a girl; whether you want a white, black, or interracial child; and whether you want a baby born in the United States or in another country.

All foreign countries and many states within the United States have their own laws and regulations concerning adoption. For example, some states do not allow independent adoptions, in which the adoptive parent locates a birth mother through her own efforts rather than going through an agency. Laws change all the time, political turnabouts in some other countries affect the procedures, adoption practices vary greatly depending upon the rules or laws of the source from which you choose to adopt, and there are many different scenarios possible whatever method you choose. The experiences of SMCs in our group have ranged from the fairly straightforward with occasionally rocky roads along the way to the very dramatic. Start by consulting your state regulatory office and a local support group in order to familiarize yourself with the state laws that will affect your situation.

The cost of adoption varies tremendously depending upon the route you choose, ranging from under one thousand dollars (rare) to fifty thousand dollars. At the very least, you will have to pay an adoption lawyer. In addition, you may have to pay support money for the mother's living expenses during her pregnancy, fees to the orphanage, the mother's and baby's medical costs, transportation costs, and support money for the care of the baby after it is born if you are adopting from a foreign country. On the other hand, if you adopt a hard-to-place (older or handicapped) child from a public agency, you may be eligible for subsidies or financial aid from your state.

Fortunately, there are many wonderful adoption support groups, even some especially for singles, that will be glad to help you learn how to work your way through the incredible amount of information and choices and will keep you abreast of changes. Nearly every SMC I know who adopted said that the crucial factor that made it all possible was her support group. (See Appendix B for a list of adoption support groups. There are also many excellent books on the subject in Recommended Reading, page 227, and the Internet also has a wealth of information on the subject.)

MYTHS ABOUT SINGLE-PARENT ADOPTION

Until a few years ago it was considerably more difficult for a single person to adopt than it is now, and many people erroneously think that it is still that difficult or even that it is not possible at all. Another widely held myth is that a single person cannot adopt a healthy infant born in the United States and can only expect to get an older child or a handicapped or foreign-born baby. In fact, a single woman can adopt a new-born baby from either the United States or abroad. The requirements are information, determination, patience, and persistence, plus a certain amount of luck, and with that you should eventually get the baby you want. Remember that some state laws prohibit independent (nonagency) adoptions, and laws regarding adoption vary from state to state, so consult with a local lawyer who is experienced with adoption and especially with a local adoption support group for information about the laws in your state.

SOME CONSIDERATIONS ABOUT ADOPTION

You may prefer to adopt rather than conceive a child because adoption has some definite advantages. For example, when you adopt you can choose the sex and the age of your child. You may not want to go through a pregnancy alone or perhaps you might have a physical condition that would be adversely affected by a pregnancy. You may not want to have to deal with the negative reactions or disapproval you may encounter from some people if you are single and pregnant. You may feel that you do not want to bring another child into the already overpopulated world in which we live, and you may instead want to provide a home for a child already born who needs one. If you adopt an older child rather than a newborn, you will be able to get a fairly good idea about who the child is since there will be lots more information available about an older child's functioning, personality traits, and strengths and weaknesses than can be known with a newborn. This is helpful if you feel the need to know what sort of child you will be living with.

Many SMCs who have adopted felt, for reasons such as those mentioned above, that this was the way they were most comfortable becoming a single mother, and that adoption was the best choice for them. Others chose to adopt after realizing that they were not able to conceive a child, and these women had to go through a second phase of grieving. First, like all SMCs, they had to grieve over the loss of the dream of having a child within a marriage to a loving spouse, and then they had to grieve again for the biological child they were not able to conceive. Both of these losses can be painful and difficult to bear, but it is essential to work through them if you want to be able to accept the kind of family with which you end up and feel genuinely good about it.

ADOPTION ISSUES

If you are thinking of adopting, you will face some different issues from those of an SMC who conceives her biological child. The most important of these have to do with the unknowns that are almost always a part of any adoption. Motherhood itself involves taking a leap into some scary territory, and single motherhood is even more scary. When you adopt you are taking what many people consider an even greater risk because there may be so much that happened in the child's life before you met him that you will never know about.

When you are carrying your biological child, you have control over what you eat and drink and have some knowledge of your family's genetic endowment, although you may or may not have that information about the father. You know almost everything that happened to your child from the moment you conceived him until you leave the hospital with him. If you are adopting, and particularly if you are adopting an older child, you may or may not have information about some of these things. With an older child there may be large gaps in the history that is available to you, but on the other hand, as mentioned above, you can see or evaluate some of his characteristics, such as intelligence, personality traits, and physical conditions, which may not be known with a newborn.

We have learned a great deal in recent years about the importance of prenatal care and notably the damaging effects that maternal alcohol consumption and smoking can have upon the developing baby. You can try to screen prospective adoptive mothers by asking about their prenatal care and their personal habits, but you are never going to be sure of exactly what they did. If your child was in a foster home or orphanage for months or years before you adopted him, his caretakers can give you a lot of information about how he functioned during that time, but they may not have much information about what his life was like before they knew him. He may have been lucky enough to have had good care in his early life or he may have been neglected or abused.

Some adoptive mothers feel more comfortable adopting an older child from another country rather than from the United States because in many countries the children are relinquished for adoption simply because of poverty, while in the United States there is often a history of emotional or physical abuse or neglect prior to an adoption plan being made for the child, and therefore sometimes the older American children have more emotional scars. On the other hand, whatever country the child is from, she may have lived in an abusive or neglectful situation, so always make sure that you are given as much example of how adoption support groups can help you. It is likely that several of the members will have worked with different adoption resources, and you can benefit from their experience in knowing which sources are more reliable and trustworthy and which ones should be avoided.

With your biological child, while you have all the information that there is to be had, there are still no guarantees that your child will not be born with or develop a problem such as a learning disability or a physical handicap. No one is guaranteed a perfect baby. However, there is some evidence that more than the average expectable number of adopted children have turned out to have problems, and in particular, attention deficit hyperactivity disorder (ADHD). ADHD is found in about 10–15 percent of the general population but some estimates state that it has been diagnosed in about 25–40 percent of adopted children.* This overrepresentation has also been noted by the adoptive parents in some of the Single Mothers by Choice chapters I have visited. The experts on ADHD speculate that this is either genetic (ADHD is, to some degree, inherited) and/or possibly related to many other factors such as poor prenatal care and diet, over which adoptive mothers have no control. Some adoption experts disagree with these statistics and believe that they are being exaggerated, or that children have been misdiagnosed, or that the incidence in the general population is being underreported.

Another issue to be aware of, particularly if your child was in an orphanage, is the possibility of what is called an attachment disorder, which results from inadequate caretaking in the early months.

---

*This is discussed in Roberts, Colleen, "Gifted Kids with Attention Deficit Hyperactivity Disorder," *OURS*, September/October 1992, pp. 22–25.

Some think that adoptive parents may be more likely than biological parents to seek help for their children because they may be economically better off than the general parent population or perhaps more familiar with the availability of helping resources as a result of having gone through the adoption process, and are therefore causing such problems to be over-reported in adoptive children. Whatever the reason, this is mentioned as an example of why it is extremely important to be both realistic and honest with yourself about what kind of child you can love. No child comes with a guarantee of perfection, and it is important that you think through what, if any, limits you may have in your ability to accept the physical, intellectual, or emotional difficulties your particular child may have.

AGENCY OR INDEPENDENT ADOPTION?

There are two kinds of adoption agencies, public and private. With either, you can adopt a baby, a toddler, or an older child from within the United States or from abroad. Many singles adopt through public or private agencies, and others choose independent private adoption through an intermediary such as an adoption attorney because they feel it offers them more flexibility and a greater number of choices. If you locate a birth mother yourself you would then contact an adoption agency, which would act as an intermediary, or you can go to a lawyer to take you through the legal steps toward finalizing the adoption. It is essential that the intermediary you use be someone who is ethical and whose reputation you have been able to check out with others. Adoption support groups (such as those listed in Appendix B) are good places to get recommendations for reliable intermediaries.

Not all adoption agencies will work with single women, but the number is growing as acceptance of single adoption is increasing. There are some agencies that will work with you if you want a healthy infant. If you are interested in a hard-to-place child (an older, interracial, or handicapped baby or child), even more agencies will work with you. Some agencies feel that a single-parent home is the best choice for a child with special needs, a physical or emotional handicap or disability, since the child will probably get more attention from a single parent than it would in a larger family where there are more demands upon the mother. Others disagree, feeling that special-needs children often need more attention than any one parent can give them.

You can usually find out if an agency works with single women by writing and asking for their brochure or by simply calling and asking some questions. Most agencies have a clearly defined policy about what qualifications they require of the prospective adoptive parents, and they are glad to answer questions. Some even have orientation meetings for the public at which they explain their various regulations, how their agency works, and what options are available (e.g., they may have only infants, or children of all different ages, or perhaps children from one particular country, or children from a variety of countries). If they say they work with both singles and couples, you still may want to ask for more specifics, such as whether singles are eligible to adopt newborns or only older children, and whether there is an agency policy on this matter or if it is left up to the birth mother to decide whether she is comfortable with a single woman adopting her baby.

Marital status is sometimes not a very important factor in the birth mother's decision, and many single women have been successful in dealing with agencies. The wait may be long, but not necessarily so if you are dealing with a relatively new agency without a long waiting list. It is even more rapid if you are willing to be flexible about the sex of the baby and the possibility of an interracial baby or one with a slightly mixed ethnic background (you may be offered a baby with one-eighth African-American background who is considered to be "mixed," for example). Some agencies may not be completely honest with you about their policy with regard to single-parent adoptions. If it is important to you to adopt an infant, be sure that you make that clear to the agency and that you are not being accepted onto their waiting list only to sit there while they offer you older children or toddlers. Ask them how many infants they have placed with single applicants, for example, and see what they say. If they are an established agency but have never given a baby to a single person, ask them why not. Perhaps they are not being totally honest.

Sometimes agencies have age requirements, such as not allowing more than forty years difference between the ages of the parent and child, and others have no such rule, so this is something else you should ask about, particularly if you are near or in your forties.

In an agency adoption the agency acts as an intermediary between you and the biological mother and father and, in a foreign adoption, between you and the other country's representatives. You may have no direct contact with the biological parent(s) or some or a lot, depending upon the agency regulations. In an independent adoption it is up to you or an intermediary to locate potential biological parents, while in an agency adoption the agency finds biological parents who wish to or need to make an adoption plan for their children. Many agencies will work with you and the biological parent(s) throughout the adoption process until the adoption is finalized and possibly afterward in order to help ensure that everyone is adjusting well. In an independent adoption there may or may not be any professional counseling built into the process. Some people believe that if there is no counseling, this makes an independent adoption less desirable than an agency adoption.

Agencies have a reputation for taking forever to give you a child. They can take a long time if they have a long waiting list, but not all agencies have such a long list. SMCs may worry that they are not being given the same treatment as couples in relation to the time spent on the waiting lists or the particular babies they will be offered because they may be judged less desirable by either the agency or the birth mothers. There may be some truth to this, depending upon the agency, and if it is the case it is usually something that rapidly becomes known within the single-adoption network. Your best bet may be a relatively new agency, which might not have any waiting list at all or have a fairly short one—at least until the word gets around through the adoption networks, after which the new agency, too, will quickly develop a long list. An adoption support group usually is current on the newest resources and which agencies are taking applications from singles, as well as how long their waiting lists may be, and can help find reputable intermediaries for independent adoption. (See Appendix B, "Single-Parent Adoption Resources.")

OPEN OR CLOSED ADOPTION?

The term "open adoption" refers to a continuum of options that enables birth parents and adoptive parents to have information about and communication with one another before or after placement of the child or at both times.* Adoptions vary in their "openness." Some adoptive mothers want to ensure confidentiality of their identity whereas others want to meet the biological parent(s) and exchange information about one another. There may be as much or as little exchange of information as the two parties are comfortable with, but regardless of the extent of the openness, the birth parents legally relinquish all parental claims and rights to the child. The strongest proponents of open adoption believe that when someone adopts, she is taking a child into her family who has another set of parents, and that this is a part of the child's situation that the adoptive parent(s) have to be prepared to accept and work with rather than pretend that there is only one family. Advocates of closed adoption believe that a child's adjustment depends upon there being a minimum of confusion and feel that the child is best off only having to deal with one set of parents.

In the past virtually all adoptions were closed. Sometimes the adoptive parents were even encouraged to not let their child know that she was adopted until she was near adulthood for fear that the information would be harmful to the child's sense of belonging in the family. As we have learned from studies of adopted children, the reverse is true: children who are *not* told the truth about their origins early in life have a more difficult time accepting and adjusting to the situation later on. When the fact that they were adopted was kept quiet, children often sensed that there was some kind of secret in their families that, it seemed, was too terrible for their parents to tell them. When they found out the truth, they often felt

*Siegal, Deborah H. "Open Adoption of Infants: Adoptive Parents' Perception of Advantages and Disadvantages." *Social Work*, 38 (1), January 1993.

betrayed and their sense of trust in their parents was severely damaged. Because we now better understand why a child needs to know the truth about her origins at an early age, adoption experts and agencies these days feel strongly that adoptive families should tell their child that she was adopted and should talk about it in front of and with the child from the earliest possible time.

While there may be no secrecy today about the fact that a child was adopted, in a closed adoption there is still confidentiality and secrecy about the identities of the biological parents, at least until the child is eighteen. One reason often given for keeping the biological parents' identities secret is to protect the child from feeling torn between two sets of parents as she is growing up. The adoptive parent(s) may also want to avoid any possibility of having to compete with the biological parent(s) for the child's loyalty and sense of identity. Advocates of closed adoption believe that the withholding of information is not a problem because once the child is old enough to decide for herself whether or not she wants to know the birth parents, she can then try to find out who they are.

In an open independent adoption both the adoptive and biological parent(s) are able to exchange whatever amount of information about one another that they are comfortable with. They may know everything about one another, including names and addresses, or may only have first names and no idea of where they reside. Some rely solely on their appointed intermediary for all communication, but others elect to meet one another and develop a relationship that may even include being in the delivery room together during the birth and keeping in touch afterward.

The purpose of their meeting is multifaceted. First, it can help the biological parent(s) feel comfortable with the new home that the baby is going to have. The adoptive parent(s) may hope that if the biological parent(s) like and are comfortable with them, there is less likelihood that they will change their minds and decide not to surrender the baby. Second, it can help to prevent the biological parent(s) from having terrible doubts afterward about whether or not they did the right thing. By knowing more about the adoptive parent(s) they have a greater degree of control over the decision about whom their child is given to and, therefore, often feel more comfortable with the whole process.

An SMC, like a married couple, may not want the biological parent(s) to have her full name or be able to contact her directly after the adoption because she may fear the birth mother will get in touch with the child years later if she decides she wants contact with him. The married couple may also fear the mother or father returning and making a claim on the child's affections or even trying to get custody (although this rarely happens despite the great amount of media attention that is generated when it does). But an SMC may have a unique fear. As one SMC said to me, "What if the birth mother gets married and then feels guilty that she let a single woman adopt her baby? She might try to get custody." You should know that once an adoption is finalized, a birth mother *cannot* change her mind and reclaim her child. (The same fear is sometimes troublesome to SMCs who have conceived with a man they knew. They worry that the father could come back at any time and try to get custody of his child, which would be his legal right. Although it is legal, in fact it is rare that a father does return after not having been involved for many years.) Depending upon how comfortable you feel about ongoing contact, there may be none or there may be exchanges of photos or notes for years, either directly or through an intermediary.

For the adoptive parent, meeting the biological parent(s)

gives some sense of the baby's heritage. You have a chance to get an idea of what the baby's parent(s) are like and whether or not you feel comfortable adopting a baby with these origins. On the other hand, there is the risk that, if the parties do not get along with one another, the adoption may not be workable.

It is sometimes reassuring to the adoptive parent(s) to see that the biological mother is a responsible person who is genuinely concerned about her baby having a caring home and that she made an adoption plan for her baby of her own volition and free will. Some adoptive parents suffer from guilt feelings about having taken a child away from his mother or worry that the mother was somehow coerced and will later try to reclaim the child.

The degree of openness in an adoption has an important impact upon the child's future relationships with both sets of parents. Some parents feel that having a minimal but ongoing relationship with the birth mother throughout the child's life protects the child from feeling that he was rejected by the birth mother. Other parents believe that this is too confusing for the child. They want it to be clear to the child that the adoptive family is *the* family and that the biological mother's role was simply that—biological. And so they discourage contact with the birth parent(s) or keep it to a minimum.

Some adoptive parents feel threatened by the possibility that if the child knows and has a relationship with the biological parent(s) he will someday ultimately prefer the biological parents and reject the adoptive parents. This may be a particular issue for an SMC who is worried that her child will miss having a dad and thus want to find and get close to his biological father. Of course, if the child wants to find his biological mother, competitive feelings can be an issue for an SMC, just as with a married mother.

Statistics compiled by the National Council for Adoption indicate that only between 2 and 5 percent of birth mothers and adoptees search for one another, although this is merely an estimate and may not be accurate. If the biological parents are willing to be located they can register with a mutual consent registry, which makes the search a fairly easy process in those states that have one (Arkansas, California, Florida, Idaho, Indiana, Louisiana, Maine, Maryland, Michigan, New Hampshire, New York, Ohio, Oregon, South Carolina, South Dakota, Texas, Utah, and West Virginia). Even if the state doesn't have a registry, it may be willing to release identifying information when there is mutual consent (Delaware, Iowa, Kansas, Massachusetts, New Mexico, Vermont), and some will allow a search through an intermediary (Alabama, Arizona, Colorado, Connecticut, Georgia, Hawaii, Illinois, Kentucky, Minnesota, Missouri, Nebraska, North Dakota, Pennsylvania, Tennessee, Washington, Wisconsin, and Wyoming). There are also search groups that are often able to locate the biological parents, sometimes to the parents' dismay. (Be aware that some search groups can be wonderful, but others are close to cults in their fanaticism about their belief that every child *must* meet his biological parents.) There are only three states that permit adoptees over eighteen to get their original birth certificates without mutual consent by the birth parents (Alaska, Kansas, and Tennessee). In all other states, mutual consent is required to obtain the original document.

Those adoptees who do not do a search often choose not to for a variety of reasons. Some say that they never had any curiosity or felt any other need to find their biological parents. Others say they were curious but didn't want to risk hurting their adoptive parent(s), whom they were worried would feel insulted or threatened if they tried to do a search. If a child was adopted from a foreign country, in most cases there is little or no likelihood of finding the birth mother.

It is also true that while the growing trend is to be as open and honest as possible with the child concerning the facts about his birth parents, some adoptive parents are extremely fearful of their child doing a search and meeting her birth parents. If that is the case it is often because they are concerned that meeting the birth parents may be very upsetting or too difficult for the child to handle, particularly if a birth parent is a very unstable or disturbed person.

The reasons that children try to find their biological parents may vary in the details, but one thing repeatedly comes through in the literature about this matter: they want to have more of a sense of identity and a connection with their biological roots, partially in order to understand themselves better but also to have some idea of what genetic endowment they will be passing on to their own children. As scientists learn more and more about the role and influence of biology on all our behaviors, it is apparent that a large percentage of who we are comes from our absorbing the characteristics of the people with whom we live, but a significant amount definitely comes from our genetic inheritance. The adopted adult may feel that it is his right to have information about this part of his biological inheritance.

Some people believe that if there is a good emotional fit between the adoptive parent(s) and the child, the child may not feel as strong a desire to find out about her biological roots as in those instances where there was clearly not an easy or successful fit between the adoptive parent(s) and child. This is not necessarily always the case, however. In some families where there wasn't a particularly good fit the child still may not feel comfortable telling her adoptive parents that she wants to find her biological parents for fear of hurting their feelings. And even where there was an apparently good fit, some adoptees just want to have as much information about their origins as possible, especially as they approach marriage and the creation of their own families.

What Kind of Adoption Is Right for You?

As you contemplate adoption, try and see what scenarios come to mind. Are you apprehensive when you hear about open adoptions or does the idea relieve some of your anxieties? Do you feel you would welcome an intermediary? Do you want minimal or no involvement with the biological parent(s)? Or do you feel strongly that the more you know about the biological parent(s), including meeting them and getting to know them personally, the more comfortable you will be with the adoption? The answers to these questions will show you the way toward the better method of adoption for you. If you do not have a preference, then you can try either approach, perhaps picking the one that looks as if it will be faster or less costly. Remember that the fact that you are a single person is *not* necessarily a major problem. You can look forward to being able to succeed with adoption if you are determined and persistent, and especially if you are working with an adoption support group to keep you up to date.

SHOULD YOU ADOPT A NEWBORN, A TODDLER, OR AN OLDER CHILD?

The prenatal care, genetic endowment, origin, and age of the baby or child when you adopt will have a great impact on who that child is and becomes. We are all shaped initially by genetic endowment and prenatal care and subsequently by the circumstances of our birth, postpartum care, and environment. As previously discussed, with your biological child you have the most information possible because you were part of his life from the moment of conception. You know all that can be known about the physical and emotional events that have shaped that child. With an adopted newborn, there may be many things you know, or you may know nothing about its origins (if the child was abandoned, for example).

The older the child at the point of adoption, the more that has happened to that child. How much of that experience you learn about depends, of course, on how much is known to the source from which you adopt the child, and also how much they choose to share with you. That is why you should try to whatever extent possible to ascertain that your resource for the adoption is ethical and reliable. But remember that even if the resource is a most reliable person or agency, they may not have been given full or accurate information about the child.

The earlier in its life you adopt a baby or child, the more information you will have as well as the greater opportunity to influence the child's development with your style of mothering. However, keep in mind that you cannot adopt a baby (or give birth to a baby for that matter) with the assumption that you will be the primary factor in shaping the baby's personality. Babies come with predetermined temperaments and capabilities, and you can influence them to some degree, but the old theory that newborns are blank slates is no longer considered valid by child development professionals.

Some women are more able to go with the flow and take a chance on any newborn without needing to know very much about his origins and history, and others feel that they cannot tolerate not knowing all there is to know. If you are someone who really wants a lot of information, that may rule out your doing a foreign adoption where there is usually less information available.

Some people want only to adopt an older child because they do not want to deal with the stresses of having an infant. They want to start off with a school-aged child who is relatively independent, and they feel that this requirement outweighs whatever degree of concern they may have about the child's early years. You may be lucky enough to find a toddler or older child who has been cared for in a loving home and has developed well, in which case you may be getting a relatively well-adjusted child. But keep in mind that an older child who has been abused or neglected can be at least as demanding as an infant. If your child has suffered trauma in her early months or years you can expect her to need a greater than average amount of emotional nurturance throughout her life—and possibly professional help as well.

U.S. OR FOREIGN ADOPTION?

Foreign adoptions can be very complex or fairly simple depending upon the specific country's policies and factors like how stable the country is during the time that you are dealing with its representatives in the adoption process. You may, as did one SMC I know, get caught in the middle of a political upheaval and find that most of the rules that you had so scrupulously followed have changed and that, in fact, this particular country is no longer permitting single parents to adopt. Or you may have no problems, find that everything goes smoothly, and come home with the perfect baby for you.

In general, adoptions within the United States tend to be less complex in terms of paperwork and bureaucratic procedures.

Even if you are adopting a newborn, in a foreign country you typically will not be able to take the baby right home immediately after his birth. If you have the flexibility to take off the time from work, you might be able to stay in the country from which you are adopting and care for the baby there while you are waiting for the paperwork and administrative proceedings to be completed. (It can take anywhere from a few days to several months depending upon the country.) If you cannot be there, the baby is usually placed in a foster home, and you will pay for his living expenses there. If you adopt in the United States you will often be able to take the baby right home, sometimes straight from the hospital nursery, even though the adoption may not be legally finalized for another several months or more.

In any adoption, there is always the agonizing fear that the birth mother might change her mind at the last minute. When it does happen, and it has happened to several SMCs I have known, it is very much like going through a miscarriage (see the sections on miscarriage in Chapter 4). But, on the bright side, every SMC I know who went through the heart-wrenching experience of having a birth mother change her mind eventually ended up with a baby, and one with whom she was thrilled.

There are many very wonderful stories about successful adoptions and there are also some very scary horror stories about tragic and disappointing situations. Both are frequently shared with great excitement among potential adoptive parents in order to either inspire or teach a little about what to be careful of. Unfortunately, the media give a lot more attention to the negative stories about adoption, and many people have real prejudices about adoption. Below are an account of the positive adoption experience of one of our SMC members, and also the story of another woman's more negative experience.

Melissa

Melissa had tried unsuccessfully to conceive for several years and finally, at age forty, she decided that enough was enough. With the help of RESOLVE, a national support group for couples and singles with fertility problems, she spent some time grieving for the loss of her dream of having her biological child and then moved fairly quickly to familiarize herself with the adoption options. She went to adoption and single-mother support groups for several months, learning a great deal about other people's experiences and clarifying her own needs.

She decided that she wanted to adopt a newborn baby, and preferably one that would be similar to her as far as racial and religious origins. She felt that this would help her in the bonding process and would also help her relatives to bond with the baby. She applied to an agency in the United States that she knew was willing to work with singles, and which several of the other single adoptive moms she knew had used, and she was put on their waiting list along with other singles and couples. This agency treats both single and married applicants exactly the same during the application phase and it gives the birth mother the right to choose the adoptive parent(s) based on profiles of the applicants that include their occupation, income, reasons for wanting to adopt a child, and other personal details.

Like most agencies, the one Melissa used matches the adoptive parents' and birth parents' racial heritage unless the adoptive mother specifically states she is open to or requests a baby from a different background. About ten months after she had completed the preliminary paperwork, the agency called Melissa and she flew to meet her baby. It was the cutest baby she had ever seen in her life (as all of our babies turn out to be)! Melissa was thrilled with her baby girl, and now, almost three years later, she is the mother of a second baby from the same agency.

Harriet

Harriet, a forty-year-old teacher of handicapped children, decided to adopt a child from another country because she wanted to give a home to a child who might otherwise spend his life in an orphanage. She had a home study done and did all the necessary paperwork to go with her application to an intermediary, an attorney in a Central American country. The attorney accepted her application, and she was told that she would be getting a call from him in approximately three months. She knew she would have to spend several weeks in that country until the legalities there were completed, and so she had arranged that the adoption would take place during her summer vacation. That way she would have the time to stay with the child while waiting for permission to take him or her out of the country and then to make the adjustment to being a new mother back home while still on vacation.

When the call came from the attorney, she was very excited, packed up her collection of baby clothes and supplies, and flew to meet her new baby. She arrived in the country and was able to meet the beautiful baby girl right away. While she was waiting for the paperwork to be processed, the country's legislature passed a law prohibiting babies from being adopted by citizens of other countries. To her horror, she was not permitted to continue with the adoption. Harriet was shattered, having already fallen in love with her baby daughter. She was fortunate that the attorney was able to help her find a contact in another country and she was able to adopt from that country very quickly, so she managed to have her new baby home before the end of that summer vacation. Although Harriet is very thrilled with the wonderful baby that she adopted, her eyes still tear when she talks about the first baby, and she knows it will take her a while to get over that loss.

BE HONEST WITH YOURSELF ABOUT WHAT YOU WANT

If you are thinking of adopting, you may feel that because you are single you have to compromise on some of your criteria for what sort of baby or child you want. This is *not* necessarily the case. You need to do some serious thinking as to whether or not you have strong preferences about what age child you want, what sex, from what country, what race, and what sort of future relationship (or lack thereof) you want with the child's biological parent(s). Some SMCs are very flexible and don't have much concern about these particulars. They want to mother a child, and that is basically the only requirement they have. Others are much more specific about their needs, either only wanting a baby that looks like them and their family or, alternatively, only wanting a baby who comes from an impoverished country in which parents sometimes cannot afford to raise their children themselves because there are insufficient resources and limited opportunities for even a minimally good quality of life. When you adopt a child from a situation such as this, whatever you have to offer is a plus and you may feel less guilty about what you cannot provide—a great deal of money or a daddy, for example.

You need to be realistic about the community in which your

child will be growing up. If you adopt a baby from another culture, are there others from that culture in your community who can help your child learn about her background, or do you live in a homogeneous community in which she will feel somewhat alone? If her racial background is different from yours, will she be accepted in your town as she grows up, attends the local school, and eventually starts dating? Is the community a multicultural one so she can easily find others who look like her? If she will not look like you, she will feel somewhat different, but if there are lots of other people around who look like her, that is less of an issue.

Some SMCs want to have ongoing contact with the biological parent(s) and others do not wish to have any contact or are only willing to have contact until the adoption is completed. Any of these preferences is fine. The most important thing is that you be clear and honest with yourself about what you want.

I have occasionally seen women in my workshops who were stuck in the midst of the adoption process, immobilized for no apparent reason. As we talked, it would sometimes become apparent that they were stuck because, in one respect or another, they were not doing what they really wanted. Perhaps they really only wanted an infant but thought that was an impossible dream for a single woman and did not even try to ask an adoption agency or lawyer about it. Then, thinking that they would only be able to adopt an older child, they were unable to follow through. Similarly, some women only want a child of their race, but feel uncomfortable saying so for fear that they will sound racist. Since this child will be a major part of your life for many years to come, it is important that you make sure that you know—and admit to yourself—what is important to you, as only this way will you get the child that you really want. And, of course, it may be that you really only want to raise a child with a loving partner and just cannot compromise your value system on that issue. If so, it is important that you listen to and respect your feelings. Single motherhood is not for everyone.

If you are not sure that you can ever love an adopted child in the same way you could love your biological child, how strongly do you feel this? It is true that some women cannot bring themselves to adopt for that reason. If that is the case with you, give yourself time to think it through and try talking to a counselor and to other mothers who have adopted. Many adoptive parents have had such fears, but most say that they start to bond with their babies just as quickly as a biological mother does. (Keep in mind that a biological mother does not necessarily bond with her baby immediately; it can be a matter of hours, days, weeks, or even months.) However, if this is a very strong feeling, and if you have made a sincere effort to understand and resolve it with no success, then perhaps adoption is not for you. Most adoption support groups will welcome you even if you are at the very beginning of the "thinking" stage and have not yet decided whether adoption is right for you. Regardless of whether or not you ultimately decide to adopt, you owe it to yourself to explore the possibility and give this decision serious thought.

Read About Adoption!
One last thought about adopting: what I have written here is only a brief summary of some of the issues and decisions involved in contemporary adoption. If you are considering this option at all seriously, I recommend strongly that you get several good books on adoption (see page 227 for a recommended reading list) so you can get an overview of the various

options and the situations that you may face. There is a great deal of excellent literature on single-parent adoption and adoption in general. Many adoptive parents have written about their own personal stories, as have a number of adopted children. There are also adoption resource books and books on the subjects of foreign versus domestic adoption, agency versus independent adoption, newborn versus older children, and open versus closed adoption, and also ones that cover the question of searching for birth parents. You can learn a great deal from the many wonderful books available. And as mentioned before, do get in touch with a couple of adoption support groups. A list of them can be found in Appendix B.

Besides those listed in Recommended Reading, you may want to call Tapestry Press at (800) 535-2007. They will send you a wonderful free catalog of books on adoption and infertility.

PART TWO

———

Being a Single Mother
by Choice

4

· ·

PREGNANCY, BIRTH, AND
POSTPARTUM

You did it! After giving it considerable thought and deciding that you wanted to become a single mother, now you are pregnant.

How do you feel? Are you shocked, excited, thrilled, frightened, sad? A combination of all these feelings? It's no wonder. Pregnancy is one of the peak experiences of a woman's life. As a girl, most likely you had exquisite fantasies about being pregnant that included a handsome, devoted, loving spouse and an abundance of relatives and friends who were joyously celebrating this blessed event with you. Even happily married women usually find that reality doesn't live up to that fantasy, and for you, as an SMC, it certainly can't. To some degree, every single mother, including those who decide to adopt, has to grieve for the loss of her dream of the perfect (married) pregnancy.

You may feel alone when no one is as excited as you are about the pregnancy. Rather than being showered with congratulations by family and friends who are eager to celebrate with you, you may have some members of your family urging you to change your mind or threatening not to speak to you ever again, and some of your friends telling you that you are out of your mind!

You may be very happy and elated during your pregnancy, or you may have mixed feelings. You may be thrilled about being pregnant but wish that you were with a loving partner. You may also feel sad at times and go through periods of depression. You will have different feelings at various stages of the pregnancy, and probably no two women will feel precisely the same way. The one thing you can count on is that your feelings will fluctuate. It may be due to the normal hormonal fluctuations of pregnancy or it may be more exaggerated because of the stress of yours not being a "traditional" pregnancy, but it is perfectly normal to experience a wide and changing range of emotions.

In getting to know many SMCs around the country, I have noticed that to a large extent the degree of emotional stress they experience is directly related to how much support they have been able to establish for themselves and how alone they do (or do not) feel. You will have an easier time during your pregnancy if there are people in your life who are supportive of your decision and understand what it means to you. Friends and relatives are of course an excellent potential source of support, although in some cases they may not be able to be understanding. If that is the case, you might find that other SMCs in your area can offer more support because they can identify with what you are going through better than anyone else. (See Appendix D for a list of support groups.)

Pregnancy is different for everyone, and women who have had several pregnancies report that each one is unique. As a pregnant SMC you will have many of the same feelings as your married counterparts, but you also will have some additional stresses due to being pregnant alone and in an alternative or nontraditional manner. You may feel most alone at the poignant times, such as the moment when you feel the very first tiny flutterings of life inside you or when you are in a phase of particular harmony with and enjoyment of the pregnancy. You may feel sad that you don't have a partner who is as excited about every new sensation of the pregnancy as you are, and toward the end you may feel worried about being alone as you anticipate your water breaking and labor beginning. Some SMCs arrange to have a close friend or relative stay with them during the last couple of weeks of their pregnancy to alleviate some of their fears of going into labor alone. This is also a nice way to be able to spend some last precious "alone time" with someone you are close to before the baby arrives and makes such occasions a rarity.

You have put a lot of time, thought, and energy into making this major decision, but this does not mean that you always will feel terrific about it. You can expect your feelings to fluctuate, but the bottom line is that you have to maintain a consistently positive attitude toward yourself, especially during the stressful times. This is no time to start second-guessing or criticizing yourself for whatever imperfections or failings you may have. When you find yourself having doubts and fears, you need to remember how much work you put into making your decision and carrying it to fruition. Remind yourself that you will try your best to be a good mother but that you do not have to have the combined energy and knowledge of two parents in order to do a good job.

Remember that you do not have to know how to handle everything—married new parents don't know everything either—and that when you don't know what to do you will ask for and get help. One of the best-kept secrets about parenthood is that most new parents, single or married, feel quite inadequate and overwhelmed, and that as much as you may try to prepare, there really is no adequate preparation. All parents go through the same on-the-job (or as some call it, trial-by-fire) training.

If people you had hoped would be supportive have not yet been able to come to terms with your decision, remember that they may be better able to accept it as more time passes and they see that you are coping and happy with it. Most SMCs find that even those most staunchly opposed to their decision often come around when the baby is a reality.

TELLING PEOPLE WHO ARE CLOSE TO YOU

Whether you have already told people of your plan before you conceived, or decided to wait until after, the many people who applaud your decision and congratulate you are no problem. Just enjoy their support! More of a challenge is how to tell the people you care about whose responses might not be so positive and who you fear might even be critical or angry.

Nancy

When Nancy, pregnant at thirty-six by donor insemination, told her parents that she was going to have a baby, they were not overjoyed. In fact, her father was furious and refused to speak to her, and her mother was very upset and tried to convince her to have an abortion. Having worked very hard at making this decision and having gone through months of inseminations, hoping and praying that she would be able to conceive, Nancy was clear that changing her mind was out of the question.

She was able to keep her spirits up despite her parents' reactions because she knew that she wanted a baby very much. She found support from friends and hoped that her parents feelings would change after the baby was born. Sure enough, once Nancy had her baby, her parents turned completely around and became typical proud, doting grandparents.

When she asked them what had made them change their feelings, they said that at first they had been deeply disappointed that Nancy wasn't getting married and were worried about her ability to handle motherhood by herself. They were also concerned, they said, about what their friends would think about her having a baby "out of wedlock." After the baby was born, however, their friends' reactions suddenly seemed less important as they realized how much they wanted to share this special time with their daughter and granddaughter.

Remember that while you may be grieving about the loss of your dreams, people who are close to you may also have had dreams for you that they realize now will not be fulfilled. Those who are most upset may not be able to offer you support until after they have come to terms with their own feelings, as was the case with Nancy's parents. It is important to allow them to have their reactions while at the same time not allowing their reactions to have an overly strong effect on you. If you feel it would be easier for you, you can at first tell only people who you know will be supportive, and wait until after the first trimester or later to tell others. Some SMCs have written letters to announce their pregnancy, allowing the other people as much time and space as they need to go through their reactions in private, rather than presenting the news in a face-to-face manner. This method also protects you from having to deal with their initial reactions, which may be harsh and unnecessary for you to hear.

If you tell people whose response is negative, remind yourself that you are not responsible for how they feel. You have a right to become an SMC, and they have a right to be upset. You might tell them that they are important to you and that you hope you can remain close with them during this important time. However, it is their job to resolve their feelings. You can try to be of help to them, but you cannot do it for them. Some SMCs have found that sending a friend or relative an article about single women choosing motherhood can help to clarify some of the reasons for their choice and lay the groundwork for having a discussion about their specific situation.

Keep in mind that how you present the situation often has a significant effect on the other person's responses. You can hope, wish for, and ask others to be supportive and understanding, but you cannot demand it. Their feelings about your decision may be very different from yours and you need to allow them to have their own reactions in as nonjudgmental a manner as you would like them to have toward you.

HELPING PEOPLE KNOW WHAT TO SAY

Even in this day and age, people will very often respond to your announcement of an unwed pregnancy with shock or surprise. Unless they have been aware of your decision to become an SMC and have participated in the planning with you, even people who are usually quite progressive in their views and attitudes will most likely go through a shocked phase. One question many people have, but might be afraid to ask, is whether or not this is good news. Often you can convey this quite clearly by including that fact in your announcement to them, such as "I have some very exciting news—I'm expecting a baby!" or "I'm very happy to tell you that I have decided to become a single mother—and I am pregnant!"

In my experience there are at least four common kinds of reactions: congratulations, surprise, stunned silence, or avid curiosity. The people who congratulate you and are happy for you are a pleasure. The surprised people often just need a little time to get over their surprise, unless they are really more shocked than surprised. They can often be helped by a little reassurance from you, as I've just described. You can chat on about how happy you are and how you are fixing up the spare room for the baby and so forth until they have had a chance to regroup and congratulate you. You can also remind them, with a smile, that they should congratulate you, and this may also help them regain their social graces and some of their composure. Try to also mention your hope that they will be able to share in your happiness and be supportive of your decision so that they know you want to include them in your life as you create your new family.

The shocked and silent people are a little tougher. You need to find out whether they are seriously disapproving or worried or whether they just need some time to come to terms with the news, but it is often difficult to tell at first. You can ask if they want to hear more details or if they have any questions, and in hearing their questions you will get some clues as to what their reactions really are all about. Are they worried about you or are they disapproving from a moral point of view? If they are worried, and their reaction is originating from concern about you, you can let them know that you appreciate it, while also trying to reassure them that you feel that this decision is right for you, and that their help and support will be welcome. If they are morally disapproving, you need to find out on what their disapproval is based. If it is because your decision goes against their value system, you may be able to continue to be friends if you can respect one another's differences, but if they are judgmental and cannot refrain from criticizing you for differing from them, you may be in for some very troubling times.

For those who are full of curiosity and questions, you will need to consider ahead of time how much information you want to share. Many times people will ask you for the most intimate details, things they would never ask a married woman, because this situation is a novelty to them and they are eager to fill in as many of the missing pieces as possible. They tend to ask who the father is, how you became pregnant, how the father feels about it, and any number of other personal questions.

Remember that you can be as open or closed as you feel like being, and that you do not have to answer the exact questions that are asked if you do not want to. You may instead want to deflect questions and take the opportunity to tell people about why you made your decision to become an SMC in order to help them understand and be supportive. You may find yourself angry at their questions, knowing that they wouldn't ask a married woman such questions. You have to evaluate how close the person is to you and how important it is to you to maintain your privacy, and balance that with your interest in educating people around you about this new kind of family.

You will find that it is very helpful to talk about your feelings with supportive people. However, even close friends may be unsure of how to be most helpful. If so, tell them! Let them know what you need from them and give them an idea of what kinds of things you would like them to say to you. For example, one SMC asked a close friend, "Sometimes I worry that I won't be able to handle all the responsibility. You know me well—do you think I'll be a good mother and do a good job?" Her friend had wanted to be helpful but was a little uptight and worried about what was the right thing to say. Once she had an idea that reassurance would be appreciated, she was able to offer not only that response but many other reassurances as well. She just needed a little assistance in getting started.

TELLING ACQUAINTANCES

Many SMCs say that when their pregnancy started to show, regardless of how liberated they may have thought they were, they were shocked to find that they felt a sudden desire to wear a band on their third finger, left hand! This is another reflection of the internal script that has always linked pregnancy with marriage. Every time you look at that empty spot on your finger, you once again have to come to terms with how it feels to be alone at this special time in your life.

Whether or not you wear a ring, virtual strangers have a habit of chatting with pregnant women, sometimes even patting their bellies, and asking such questions as "How does your husband feel about the news?" or "Does your husband want a boy or a girl?" It is almost as if you have become public property. You will need to decide how to respond to these kinds of questions and what to tell people at different levels of importance in your life.

The situation with the passing stranger is perhaps easiest, because you can say whatever you want to him or her at the time and may never see the person again. Somewhat more complicated to deal with are people in your neighborhood or at work who are not close or intimate friends, but whom you see on a regular basis. When they notice that you are pregnant, they may assume that you got married. Accordingly, after congratulating you on your pregnancy they might add, "I didn't know you got married!" or "When did you get married?" Some SMCs simply dodge the question and respond to the congratulations, saying, "Thank you. I'm thrilled about it." A more sensitive person, hearing your response, may back off. Others, however, will persist in questioning you, whether out of curiosity, concern for you, or just plain nosiness.

With such people you need to decide how much information you want to make public about your situation. Do you want to sidestep the question and remain vague, or do you want to let people have some information? If you choose to respond with information, you will need to give some thought to how specific you will be in your responses.

Are you an open person in general and do you feel comfortable and happy with your decision to become an SMC? If so, you might want to tell people a little about the situation. You might simply say, "Thank you for your good wishes! I've decided to become a single mother." Or you might go into more detail, explaining that when you realized that you were getting to the end of your childbearing years you decided to go ahead and start a family alone. With the current popularity of the *Murphy Brown* TV show, often just saying, "I'm a *Murphy Brown* mom," is sufficient for many to get the picture. Some people will be interested in more details, others will be awkward or uncomfortable and drop the matter. Keep in mind that it is up to you to set the boundaries for how much or how little to say based on how much privacy you want to have.

On the other hand, you may find yourself wanting to tell everybody everything. Ask yourself why. You need to be sure that you are not reacting to feeling a little guilty or uncomfortable by overexplaining. If it comes out of genuine happiness, however, an open, upbeat attitude combined with a simple explanation helps give people a clear message that you are relaxed and pleased with your situation.

Be prepared for all sorts of reactions. Since it is still a fairly unusual phenomenon, almost everyone is curious, although some people contain it better than others. Remember that their reactions tell you a lot about them but say nothing about you. And don't be too sure that you know how people will react. You may be surprised!

Mary

Mary, who became pregnant at thirty-six by donor insemination, lived in a small, conservative community and was sure that people's responses to her decision would be very negative. She went through her pregnancy without discussing it with anyone except a few close friends and family members. Her daughter was born in November, and Christmas gifts for the baby from neighbors and acquaintances in her town started to arrive shortly thereafter. Mary was at first dumbfounded and then thrilled as more and more presents kept arriving. By Christmas Day, Mary's daughter had over forty gifts under the tree, and a few more were brought over by neighbors who stopped by on Christmas to wish them both a happy holiday! No one was more surprised than Mary, who had been prepared to be the object of much disapproval.

This example reflects something that I have often seen to be the case: people respond not only to the facts of a situation but also to who you are as a person. It was very apparent from the reactions she got that Mary was a much liked and respected person in the town, and the people in her community had found a lovely way to let her know that they were supportive of her decision.

BABY SHOWERS

If you always wanted to have a baby shower, have one! Most likely someone will volunteer to have one for you, or you can ask a supportive friend or relative to help you plan one.

Baby showers are fun, and for an SMC they can also help demonstrate to friends and family that you are happy to be pregnant and are enjoying celebrating this exciting time in your life. If some people are so uncomfortable with your decision to become a mother that they cannot join in your celebration, don't pressure them to attend the shower. They may need more time to adjust to the idea and come around later at their own speed, or they may never really be able to be supportive. It is important to allow people to deal with this somewhat unconventional decision in their own way while not allowing their reactions to influence your feelings unduly.

COMPLICATIONS OF PREGNANCY

You may have a delightful and easy pregnancy, but there is always the possibility that you will miscarry or develop medical complications. People often don't know how to relate to a married woman who has miscarried, and with an SMC they may feel even more awkward. The best advice, in my opinion, comes from women who have experienced a pregnancy loss. They say that having a sympathetic friend who was able to be there just to listen was the greatest help during their grieving.

There is always the risk of having a difficult pregnancy. You should be prepared for the possibility of medical problems before or after the delivery that may require you to be on bed rest or spend more time in the hospital than you had planned. You will need to have a financial cushion in case you are unable to work for an extended period of time and a support system that can help you with the emotional stress of medical complications.

Miscarriage of a Planned Pregnancy

Some SMCs have told me that it was only after they miscarried that they realized that despite being told otherwise, many people did not believe that the SMCs had really wanted or planned their pregnancy, but rather had assumed that it was an accident resulting from a moment of impulsiveness or recklessness. In the event of a miscarriage, these people may make comments like, "You must be so relieved," or "Perhaps it was not meant to be." What they may mean is, "I think you were making a big mistake, and you should be grateful and relieved that you got off the hook so easily."

If you had planned to become pregnant, it is infuriating and depressing to hear such unsympathetic responses. Yet you have to be prepared to hear them and to respond in whatever way feels right for you. You might let the comment pass and not respond at that moment. Or you might tell the person how you really feel. The decision is yours, but remember that you are entitled to exactly the same support, sympathy, empathy, or whatever as any other woman who has miscarried.

Try to find people to talk to who understand how much the pregnancy meant to you. If they are having a hard time figuring out what to say, help them! Even good friends can at times freeze up and become tongue-tied, especially in a situation about which there may be a complicated set of emotions, such as your pregnancy. Tell them you need empathy and someone to listen to you in a caring, nonjudgmental way. A friend who can listen well can be tremendously helpful, even if only by murmuring sympathetic noises.

Twenty percent of all pregnancies end in miscarriage, and

for most there is no discernible reason. Your doctor will tell you if a reason can be found and if there is something that can be done to prevent a future miscarriage. Once you are emotionally recovered and have medical clearance from your doctor, you can start trying to conceive again.

Miscarriage of an Accidental Pregnancy
If you miscarry an accidental pregnancy, you will need to sort through whatever feelings you had about the pregnancy and review what went into the decision to go ahead with it, as well as the consequences of that decision. If you were very ambivalent about becoming a single mother, you may find that you are relieved that you miscarried. Perhaps, then, single motherhood is not for you or the timing of your becoming a single mother was wrong.

If your accidental pregnancy resulted in the ending of a relationship with a lover, you have to decide whether or not you want to try to renew the relationship. Several questions need to be addressed as you make this decision. Who ended the relationship? How do you feel about him now? Has the door been left open so you can go back to him, and do you want to, knowing that he does not want a child? Can you be content to live without having a child or have you decided that having a child is really your priority at this time? How was he feeling about you when you split up? Was he urging you to reconsider ending it? You may also want to review "Accidental Conception" on page 46 in Chapter 2.

Perhaps you became pregnant accidentally and found you were thrilled, but then miscarried. Realizing that you wanted a baby may have been a shock at first, but now you know how very much you wanted it. You may have gone through a very difficult decision-making process about the pregnancy, weighing the relative importance to you of the relationship with your lover and your desire for a baby, coming to terms with the father's and your own reactions, and ultimately facing the fact that you really wanted to have the baby. It can be surprising to realize the depth of feeling a miscarriage can cause, especially when the pregnancy was accidental, but the pregnancy may have opened up very intense feelings about motherhood.

You will now need to think about whether an intentional pregnancy or adopting a baby is something you would like to pursue once you have physically and emotionally recovered from the miscarriage.

BEFORE GOING INTO THE HOSPITAL

You will need to decide about some important matters in advance of delivery, such as who will be your labor coach (someone who will be with you during childbirth preparation classes and help you during labor and delivery), how to fill in the "father" part of the birth certificate (which will vary depending upon your relationship with the father and whether or not he has acknowledged paternity), and who will be your baby's legal guardian should you become unable to care for him after you deliver. You should also have a will and some kind of financial insurance set up before giving birth, if at all possible.

The Need for a Coach
Labor and delivery are tough under the best of circumstances, and it is especially important for you, as an SMC, to have an emotionally supportive person with you as your coach. Ask

someone with whom you feel comfortable to be your coach. He or she must be willing to accompany you through your labor and delivery, as well as attend the childbirth preparation classes with you and practice the childbirth exercises with you at home prior to your due date. Most SMCs are able to find a friend or relative who is willing to be their coach, and sometimes members of an SMC group take the role for one another. If you are not able to find someone you know to be a coach, do not despair. Usually at least some, if not all, of the OB nurses are trained labor coaches. They tend to be terrific human beings and will be more than happy to help you during your delivery.

Childbirth Classes

You might feel a bit awkward about bringing your labor coach to the class since most of the women in the class will be with a spouse or lover. However, you may find yourself to be the only single woman in a room with ten or twenty affectionate couples, and having someone with you can be a big help. It is also important to talk to the instructor ahead of time about your being an SMC and be sure her attitude is welcoming. If she isn't supportive of you, look for other options and go elsewhere if you can. Childbirth instructors tend to be a fairly positive and progressive group of people and you should be able to find one who is right for you.

Making a Will and Appointing a Legal Guardian

We all like to think that we are immortal, but there is a possibility that you will become severely disabled or die during delivery or in the early months of your child's life. It is essential to have some kind of life insurance so that there will be immediate and ample resources to cover the care of your child by her legal guardian. Life insurance is the simplest and most liquid kind of asset you can have other than cash. It is also important to consider who you would like the baby's legal guardian to be in the event of your death or total disability, and discuss it with them. You should prepare a will before the birth that clearly spells out your wishes with regard to your estate, and in particular who you have chosen to be the baby's legal guardian. If you do not specify a legal guardian, your child may become a ward of the city or state and be put into the foster care system, something you do *not* want to happen. You should also appoint someone to have power of attorney to handle your financial and legal affairs, and to be the baby's guardian, in the event that you become severely or totally disabled.

IN THE HOSPITAL

LABOR AND BIRTH

Giving birth is different for everyone, and no two births are exactly the same, even for the same person. Yet most women have a similar reaction after giving birth, particularly the first time—they want and need to talk about it. Perhaps this is because it is an experience that is like nothing else in our lives. In our society few nonmothers have participated in or even observed a birth. There has been a trend recently to be more open about childbirth, as demonstrated by the great number of videotapes being made of births and also by the fact that more birthing centers and hospitals are allowing the presence of family members, sometimes even children, during childbirth. But for the vast majority of people, childbirth is still shrouded in mystery and not even the best childbirth class can fully prepare you for the intensity of the experience.

As a single mother you will probably not be sharing the birth with the baby's biological father. However, you will most likely have a coach or birthing partner who has attended childbirth preparation classes with you and with whom you have practiced for several weeks preceding the birth. It is very important to go over the class assignments together as often as you need to so that you feel as prepared as possible when your labor begins.

You may want to write about your labor and delivery in a diary or journal. Everyone thinks she will never forget even one detail about the experience, but in fact, everyone forgets a lot! The first few weeks or even months at home are chaotic, and in the midst of the whirlwind, you may realize that you cannot recall exactly what you said to the doctor at the moment when the cord was cut, or whatever other special moment you were sure you would never forget. If you are comfortable with pictures, by all means have your coach or a nurse take either still photos or videotapes. Nearly all hospitals are willing to cooperate with you in the picture-taking effort.

Dealing with Hospital Personnel

You may be one of the first SMCs in your area, or the hospital may already be familiar with the SMC phenomenon. If you are one of the first, some of the hospital staff may not understand what your circumstances are. Some may be very confused and you may have to educate them a bit. Be aware that they all will have their own personal reactions to your being single and that some will naturally be more supportive than others. In addition to their own feelings about your being an SMC, some staff people may give you advice and often even misinformation, so be sure to come as prepared as possible with information about the laws and procedures in your state concerning relevant matters such as filling out the birth certificate. Remember that you are probably more of an expert on single mothers by choice than they are, so consider how what they tell you compares with what you already know, and when in doubt consult a lawyer. Most of the time the advice or information offered comes from a desire to help and a concern for your well-being, as Barbara (see below) found out during her stay in the hospital.

Barbara

Barbara, a thirty-seven-year-old SMC, told me about a humorous experience she had while in the hospital. Barbara's pregnancy had been very complicated, and as she held and nursed her baby during the first few days after the birth, her eyes often filled up with tears of joy and relief that her baby had turned out to be healthy and beautiful. The head nurse, although trying to be tactful, was obviously concerned about the tears.

She finally asked Barbara if she thought she needed to see the staff psychiatrist. Barbara was shocked and mystified and asked why the nurse would suggest such a thing. "It's about your crying," the nurse replied. "We're worried that you're depressed, being alone and all." "For heaven's sake," Barbara responded, "why didn't you ask me? I'm not depressed. I'm thrilled that the baby and I got through this, and I'm crying tears of joy. I'm an emotional person and for me crying is a release." The nurse smiled with relief and said, "Great! In that case, can I bring you an extra box of tissues?"

Visiting Hours

Barbara's anecdote is a good example of a well-intentioned misunderstanding, but there may be times while you are in the hospital that are poignant or make you feel sad. Visiting hours are wonderful if you have visitors, but can be agonizingly lonely times if you do not. It is a good idea to try to space your visitors so that they are distributed throughout the days you are there to ensure that you have some company during almost all the visiting times. Also, remember that, unlike a married mother, you don't have a partner to help entertain the visitors, and you can easily get exhausted and overwhelmed if too many come at once.

Many SMCs find "fathers' visiting hours" (a time when everyone except fathers has to leave; they generally follow regular visiting hours) to be a stressful time. The couples cooing over their new babies and each other may cause you to feel especially alone. There isn't really much you can do about it except be prepared for it and try to distract yourself. Some hospitals will allow your labor coach to stay during the "fathers' hour," but you most likely will have to ask your doctor to request this on your chart. If your labor coach is a woman you may still feel a little out of sync when all the other mothers have men with them, but having someone there is better than having no one. If the hospital will not allow anyone besides the father, use that time to call a friend, take a shower, or enjoy a little private time with your baby. Or, if that's not distracting enough, get some exercise by taking a walk down the hospital corridors.

After childbirth you will probably want to share many of your feelings about the experience with your coach and also with other new mothers whom you may meet during the postpartum stay at the hospital and afterward. No one will be as interested in every detail about what you went through as you would like, but the most interested person is usually another new mom, married or single. Most childbirth preparation classes have reunions after two or three months. The reunion offers you an opportunity to compare notes and to see if there is anyone with whom you want to keep in touch. Once again, at this point you need not worry about whether the potential new friend is married or single but whether you feel good about talking with her. Having another mother to talk to during the postpartum period is one of the best gifts you can give yourself. If possible, find two or three.

HOW TO FILL OUT THE BIRTH CERTIFICATE

After the baby has been born you will have to fill out a form that will document your baby's birth. The information you give will appear on your child's birth certificate, a document that will be presented to officials throughout your child's life at such times as school or camp registration, voter registration, and if he applies for a passport. At some point your child will also see it, so whatever you put on it should be consistent with what you will be telling the child and want him to know.

The form you fill out in the hospital usually asks your name, the father's name, the date and place of your baby's birth, your age, and possibly some additional information such as whether or not you have had any other children. Particularly if you have conceived with a man you know, how you fill out the space that says "Name of Father" has serious legal implications that will affect you and your child for at least the next eighteen years and emotional implications that may last even longer. States have varying laws about how an unmarried mother should fill out the birth certificate and it is very important to check with a lawyer or your local Department of Health ahead of time to determine what the laws are with regard to birth certificates in your state.

As mentioned earlier, whatever hospital you are in may or may not have personnel who are well trained to help you with the birth certificate forms. It is important for you to be prepared for possible confusion on their part, particularly if they are not accustomed to dealing with SMCs. They may give you misinformation simply out of inexperience, or they may offer advice that is incorrect with the best intentions. Barbara, the tearful but happy SMC discussed above, was urged by a clerk in the hospital to put the father's name on the birth certificate, despite the fact that in her state she could not do so without the father having signed a notarized acknowledgment of paternity, something that he was not willing to do. Another SMC I know was advised by a nurse's aide to "give the baby the father's last name when you name her; you'll see, the father will eventually come around."

While it is true that you can give your baby any last name in the world (yes, you can name him Elvis Presley or name her Murphy Brown), you may well not want the father to "come around" if he is an abusive or emotionally unstable person. If you've conceived by DI you obviously cannot put down the father's name or give it to the child, but the hospital staff may not know how you conceived and assume there is a man out there somewhere unless you say on the form that you conceived by donor insemination. Most SMCs give the child their last name because they want their child to feel connected to them and this is one way to facilitate that.

IF YOU CONCEIVED WITH A MAN YOU KNOW

Should You Put His Name on the Birth Certificate?

Almost all SMCs who are clear that the father will not be an important figure in the child's life give their children the same last name as they have. The small percentage who have an ongoing relationship with the father and expect that the father will be a participant in the child's life usually will have worked this out with him before the birth, and if he has agreed to and filled out the legal documents acknowledging paternity, they will put his name on the birth certificate and perhaps also give the child his last name.

Sometimes an SMC who knew the father, particularly if she conceived accidentally, may want him to acknowledge paternity even if he will not be involved in the child's life at all. This may be because, like it or not, in some people's minds there is still some sense of stigma in our society about being an unmarried mother, and some single mothers feel that there is even more of a stigma if the father does not acknowledge paternity. They do not want people to draw the implication that he didn't respect or love them enough to acknowledge paternity of their child, an act that is sometimes referred to as "legitimizing" a child. They may also want the child to feel connected to his father and feel that they can foster this by the child's having the father's last name and using it in daily life, even if that is the only connection he has with the father. SMCs who feel this way tend to be more traditional in their thinking and often were initially hoping that the father would be part of their family, even in a limited way as is the case with many divorced fathers. SMCs in this kind of situation are likely to be disappointed, angry, and perhaps even ashamed about being an unmarried mother if the father does not want any involvement and does not cooperate with their wishes. If he does become part of their lives, the SMC and the father usually work out arrangements regarding visitation, support, and other important decisions similarly to a divorced family.

If an SMC actively planned and chose to become pregnant, it is unlikely that she would feel strongly that the father's name should go on the birth certificate or be given to the child. Those SMCs who actively chose to become single mothers tend to be independent and may want to let it be known that they got pregnant deliberately, either by using donor insemination or with a man, and that they are feeling strong and capable about raising a baby on their own. They also may not want to put the father's name on the birth certificate for legal reasons, as described below.

Drawbacks of Putting His Name on the Birth Certificate
You need to be aware that putting the father's name on the birth certificate opens up a hornet's nest of potential serious legal complications. For example, if you are planning on traveling outside the United States with your child and the father's name is on the birth certificate, you may not be allowed to take your child out of the country without a written statement from the father consenting to your doing so. An SMC I know was traveling to Mexico and was stopped at the border because her child's birth certificate had the father's name on it and the border patrol was concerned that she was kidnapping him without the father's consent. While this does not always happen, and it is unclear what possessed this particular border guard to question the situation, it can happen.

You also will be leaving the door wide open for the father to claim his parental rights and become involved at any time in the future if he so chooses, since putting his name on the birth certificate clearly acknowledges his paternity. If he establishes paternity he can then exercise all of the legal rights available to him as a parent in your state, exactly as if you and he had been married. He can have visitation, he can try to stop you from relocating to another part of the country or traveling outside the country, and he can sue you for custody.

IF YOU CONCEIVED BY DONOR INSEMINATION

If you have chosen to be an SMC and conceived by insemination, you may want that to be known and feel proud to put "conceived by donor insemination" where it asks for the father's name on the form. If you don't want that fact to be generally known, you have the option of letting that space remain blank, thus leaving your method of conception unclear to the various officials, such as school personnel, who will look at the document throughout your child's life. Some SMCs leave it blank out of consideration for the child, who may feel embarrassed at having this rather private information known to the various people who will be seeing it.

If you chose insemination with a known donor, you have a somewhat more complicated situation regarding the birth certificate. If you leave the father's name off the form, some of the people who see it may assume that the pregnancy was an accident, after which the father refused to take responsibility. Alternatively, some people may think that you had sex with more than one partner and do not know the identity of the father. You may not be at all concerned about what these people think about how you conceived, in which case it won't be an issue for you. On the other hand, if you put the father's name on the form, you risk the many potential serious legal complications described above. Of course, if you have written up and signed an agreement with the donor, you have already acknowledged his paternity. The two of you then can jointly decide whether or not you want his name on the birth certificate and whether the child will have his last name or yours when you are drawing up the agreement.

The Birth Certificate Is a Public Document

Generally speaking, in most states, if you conceived by donor insemination, you can either leave the "father" question blank on the form or write in "conceived by donor insemination." It is your choice and you can handle it whichever way you prefer, depending upon how much information you want the world to know. Keep in mind that the birth certificate will be a matter of public record and you should only put on it what you are comfortable sharing with the world—and, obviously, with your child.

You may want to leave it blank so that no one knows the details of your personal story unless you choose to tell them. Or, as described above, you may feel good about having chosen to use donor insemination and want to have that on the birth certificate so that people who see it will know that your pregnancy was a deliberate choice and not an accident.

The original birth certificate can sometimes be quite lengthy and detailed. Besides the parent(s)' names, it may give date, time and place of birth, and other births, if any, you may have had. If you prefer not to reveal this much, when you come home from the hospital or any time after that you can write to your local Department of Health and request a short form of the birth certificate, if available in your state. In many states the short form shows only the child's name, parent(s)' names, and the date and the place of birth. You can use either the short or the long form for school registration and other official situations if you want to maintain your privacy.

THE POSTPARTUM PERIOD—HOME ALONE

Many women feel elated after childbirth and have a dramatic burst of energy. You might feel like checking out of the hospital sooner than your doctor recommends. However, the next few weeks and months are going to be exhausting and, once you leave the hospital, you will find it difficult to get a good night's sleep for a long while. Get as much rest as you can to prepare you for the postpartum period at home and *resist* the temptation to leave the hospital any sooner than necessary.

Just as with labor and birth, few of us are really prepared for what the postpartum experience is like. Not only do we not know exactly what to expect, but even if we know it will be very overwhelming and exhausting, we really cannot imagine just how that will affect our capacity for reasoning, judgment, and many other abilities that we take for granted. We also are not accustomed to being in a constant state of chaos and enduring sleep deprivation while living with a primitive being who is (appropriately) totally self-centered and ruthless in its demands! Most of us SMCs are nearly middle-aged, used to living alone and having things our way a good deal of the time, and we take for granted a certain degree of order and predictability in our lives. Well, be prepared to throw all predictability out the window and try to learn to accept chaos as normal for a while—quite a while.

Fortunately, nearly all new mothers go through a stage that helps us cope with this situation. Called "primary maternal preoccupation," it is a state of being extremely absorbed and wrapped up in your baby, to the near-exclusion of anything else, for several months. (It is often a source of frustration to spouses, but we, as SMCs, don't have to worry about that.) When a mother is so preoccupied with her baby, the baby is assured of getting the special attention that it needs to survive while it is at its most helpless and vulnerable. This period of intense absorption also supports the mother-child bonding process and allows the mother to temporarily regress and not worry about the mundane things that might get in the way of her being maximally available to her baby during this important early time.

Some mothers think they should fight the tendency to be in this state of preoccupation, feeling overly concerned about things like the neatness of the house, or trying to prove to themselves or to the world that they are the same as always despite the demands of being a new mother. However, mothers who can relax and allow themselves to be totally absorbed in the mother-baby experience often find that they get to know and understand their baby sooner, and that ultimately the chaos does not last as long as it does with mothers who try to maintain more control.

COPING WITH THE FIRST FEW WEEKS POSTPARTUM

It is probably impossible to accurately convey in words just how chaotic a day with a newborn can be and how out of control you, as a new mother, can feel. And if I could describe it, you would probably not believe me. Shortly before I gave birth I read a book about motherhood that included a chapter which described, minute by minute, a day in the life of a mother of an infant. While I recognized how stressful the day was for that mother, it didn't have much impact on me. I simply dismissed it as irrelevant, thinking those famous last words, "*My* baby won't be like that," as well as those other famous last words, "I will handle myself better than she did." When we come across something that is too much for us to deal with, we often respond with that kind of denial to protect ourselves from freaking out. So just trust me—it is a demanding and stressful time, and you would be wise to try to do as much preparation before the baby arrives (i.e., make and freeze casserole dinners, stock up on essentials, organize your closets and drawers, and do whatever other kinds of things you can that will make life simpler for you during the first few months).

Sleep Deprivation

Your baby cannot help needing to wake up several times a night since she cannot hold enough milk to get through the eight hours you may be used to sleeping, and you may not yet have learned to get back to sleep quickly (this is a skill that you can develop which involves not letting yourself wake up fully while you are feeding the baby), and so you will suffer from sleep deprivation. Although inevitable in the early months, sleep deprivation can be a serious problem because it adds to your sense of chaos and tends to exaggerate all your emotional responses. If you need to take a nap, that is a good time for someone else to play with the baby while you catch up on a little sleep and get back some of your sense of perspective. You will be amazed to find how different things may seem when you have managed to get a decent amount of sleep.

Let People Help You

You need to make sure you have a lot of help available to you when you come home from the hospital and that you are willing to accept help. Many new mothers prefer to be the primary one to deal with the baby and have others do the shopping, cooking, or laundry. If that is your preference, that's fine, but be sure to be specific with people who offer to help as to exactly what kind of help you want and be sure to make it clear if you don't want help with the baby. Some folks may offer to help and will be willing to do whatever you need, while others really just want to hold and play with a cute little baby. Arrange for the ones who only want to help with the baby to do that while you nap or run an errand. The same advice applies when *you* ask people for help. Clarify what it is that you need them to do and be as specific as possible so that they can make a realistic decision.

Keep in mind that you can now *never* go out of the house without the baby unless the baby is in the care of someone else. Even if you leave the baby contentedly asleep, he could awaken while you are gone and panic when no one responds to his cries, and he would be totally helpless should a fire or other emergency suddenly occur. Once the baby is able to creep or crawl, you have to keep an eye on him every minute since there is no end to the amount of trouble a curious and mobile baby can get into.

The fact that babies and toddlers need constant supervision is often more of a problem for an SMC than a married mother since there is no other person to stay home with the baby during those times when you may need to run out for just a couple of minutes to pick up something. It can seem like a major expedition to do that with a baby, especially in cold weather when you have to get her all bundled up, an undertaking that may take five times longer than the errand itself. If the baby is already asleep for the night, you may not want to go because waking her at that point often means possibly several more hours before you can get her back to sleep. One of the most frustrating experiences is to get back from the store, undress the baby, unpack the groceries, and find that you have forgotten one important item and have to repeat the whole process!

Do not try to do everything yourself. If you can ask a neighbor to come in and watch the baby for five minutes so you can run out to the store while the baby is sleeping, do so. Or maybe, if you live in an apartment building, a neighbor would let you bring the baby to her place. However, this has to be someone the baby knows—he will go into terrors if he should awaken and find himself in a strange place with a stranger's face peering down at him. Another possibility is to call the store and ask if they would deliver what you need. They might charge a small fee, but it is often well worth it if you just cannot get out. Perhaps you can call a friend or relative and ask them to get you what you need. Most people are more than glad to help out in this way as long as you don't ask them to overextend themselves. Spread these kinds of requests out among as many people as possible.

During the few quiet moments you have, it is a good idea to try to anticipate what you might need during the next few days. Don't wait until the last minute to try to find someone to help. Make a list of things you need people to help you with and maintain it in an ongoing way. You then can refer to the list at those moments when someone may ask if there is anything they can do, moments when invariably your mind will go blank. If you keep this list handy, you can then look at it and see which of the things on the list are best suited to that particular person or have greatest priority.

You might be interested to know that a study done in 1988 of a group of new SMCs and new married mothers showed that during their babies' first year, the SMCs were more satisfied with their lives and with motherhood than were their married counterparts. (The SMCs in the study who were the most sure that they wanted to become single mothers and felt the most supported in their decision not surprisingly were the most satisfied with motherhood.) After the first year, the SMCs and the married mothers did not significantly differ in satisfaction level.* In my experience, many SMCs love the fact that they can devote their full attention to getting to know and adjusting to the demands of their babies. Perhaps the married women have a more conflicted situation, having to decide between the needs of their babies and their spouses, and therefore they feel more stressed.

All mothers complain about the chaos and the sleep deprivation in the first few months of motherhood, but there are positive aspects to this phase that are less often talked about. Although the middle-of-the-night awakenings and feedings are disruptive, there is a special coziness and closeness to those times, especially if you do not have to worry about having to get up the next morning to go to work. Some mothers say they wish they had been able to appreciate those special moments more at the time because once they are over, there is nothing quite like them again.

THE END OF POSTPARTUM

At some point you will find that the baby is getting into a routine, that you have some idea of what to do to soothe her, when to change her diaper, when she is hungry, sleepy, bored, or whatever. You will start to think more about yourself, want to look nicer and wash your hair more often. You will be glad to hear from friends and urge them to visit, wanting to talk with them even more than you want to attend to the baby. Congratulations! You are beginning to get yourself back.

*Perone, Julie. "Single Mothers by Choice: Transition and Decision-Making Styles." University of Maryland, Department of Counseling and Personnel Services, 1988.

Some mothers find that they start to get their sense of self back as soon as three or four months, while others so enjoy the total absorption with the baby that they may prolong it or allow it to go on for a year or two. This probably is basically a reflection of the mother's personality style, as some of us just seem to feel more comfortable in the fuzziness of a baby's world and others are more eager for orderliness to dominate. Accordingly, it is difficult to say precisely when the return to reality occurs. Ideally it is a gradual process that happens by degrees. The notable exception to this is the situation where a new mother has to return to work at a certain time because of the policies of her office rather than according to her emotional readiness.

This can be a difficult and painful phase if you are not yet feeling ready to focus on the demands of the workplace. Most people's jobs and careers call for skills that tend to be almost the opposite of those needed when caring for a new baby, and so you may feel almost like two different people during the initial weeks of your return to work. This may be even more true if you are breast-feeding or have been feeling in touch with some of the more instinctual aspects of being a new mother and then have to turn around and function on an entirely different level at the workplace.

The birth is the first separation from the baby, and the end of the postpartum phase is the second one. The birth is a physical separation but the end of postpartum is more of an emotional separation, the first of many poignant ones as the baby begins his journey toward becoming a separate person with his own thoughts and feelings.

5

. . . .

THE DADDY ISSUE

Mary, an SMC with a two-and-a-half-year-old little boy, told me one day that she found herself checking every storybook before reading it to her son to see whether or not it had the word "daddy" in it. If it did, she would put it aside and not read it to him. When I asked her why she was doing this, she said she thought that if she didn't mention the word "daddy" she could delay as long as possible the inevitable questions she feared the story might raise. She just didn't feel prepared to answer them.

One thing I should say up front is that we are learning new things about this matter every day as the children born to single mothers by choice are maturing. Whatever I say about this (or any other topic, for that matter) is not meant to be gospel, nor is it written in stone. To the contrary, it is always subject to modification and change as we learn more from our experiences. With my own child I made many mistakes and learned a great deal from them. I like to believe that none of them did any irreparable damage.

Let me tell you about one important finding that may help

you feel more comfortable as you struggle with helping your child sort out the facts of her family structure: some research is already in, as I mentioned earlier, and it indicates that children from never-married-mother homes (or SMC families, as we call them) seem to have fewer difficulties in academic and social adjustment in adolescence than children who live either with divorced mothers or in stepfamilies.* This is good news for us because it suggests as I have suspected all along, that the stability of our homes is more of a factor in helping our children to grow up well than the number of parents in the home. As more research comes in, and if it continues to show these kinds of results, it will surely help us to be less anxious, less worried, less guilt-ridden, and more positive about the fact that single motherhood is a viable way to create a family and raise well-adjusted children.

However, your child inevitably will go through periods of confusion about "the daddy issue" and if you are prepared for this you can be a great help to him.

PREPARING FOR THE DADDY QUESTIONS

The subject of what to tell our children about their fathers is by far the biggest concern of single mothers by choice. Like most important and complex subjects, this one needs a considerable amount of preparation on your part to enable you to lay the groundwork for its discussion with your child. The way you handle the question "Do I have a daddy?" will reflect your view of the world, a view that you may or may not even be aware of, and that you present to your child every day, even

---

*Demo and Acock. "Family Structure and Adolescent Behavior."

before he or she can speak. In addition, the way you deal with this issue also says a great deal about how you feel about your decision to have become a single mother and about the circumstances of your child's conception. The end result of your preparation, ideally, is that you will be able to answer your child's questions about his dad (or more accurately, the lack thereof) in a positive way that will help him accept and feel comfortable with his family situation.

Perhaps the most important issue that underlies the daddy questions for an SMC is that by having a child outside of a marriage you now are part of what society considers an "alternative family," whereas previously you may have seen yourself as a fairly traditional person who was a part of the mainstream culture. You may even have been somewhat uncomfortable with or disapproving of others who were different from yourself, having either the more common prejudices toward homosexuals or people of other races or, on a more subtle level, negative feelings about people who have different values or preferences of which you disapprove. If so, you will need to do some really hard thinking and attitude adjusting, because now some people will be looking at you and your child in a judgmental and critical way. You cannot criticize someone else for being different and then not expect that your child will feel bad at some point about being different. If you have come to feel positive or at least neutral about the concept of being different yourself, you will then be in a position to teach your child to appreciate each person's uniqueness and to be accepting of differences. At some point you will be telling your child that there are all different kinds of families and you will want your child to hear that as a positive thing.

It may help to keep in mind that there are now more alternative families, including stepparent families, single-parent families, gay and lesbian families, and unmarried couples living together, than traditional nuclear families in the United States, so the alternative family is actually *more* typical rather than less. U.S. Census Bureau statistics indicate that only about 22 percent of all families today are traditional families. Our attitudes toward these various kinds of families have been shaped by our own upbringings and family history, and some of your own prejudices can't help but be stirred up and will surely be communicated to your child as you try to answer his questions. Most important, though, is maintaining and communicating your conviction that a family does not have to fit the traditional model in order to be acceptable.

Resolve Your Own Feelings

It is important to try, if you possibly can, to resolve whatever anger or disappointment you may have about the circumstances of your child's conception before she is old enough to start asking questions. That way, when the questions start, you can respond to and hear the *child's* needs rather than respond out of your own conflicted feelings, and you can be relatively neutral in tone and positive in the interpretation of the facts. Talk about it with friends and anyone else who will listen, and if you are not able to get beyond your upset feelings, go for counseling. You owe it to your child.

How do you know whether or not you have worked out your feelings? Typical indications that you have *not* are a tendency to avoid using the words "daddy" or "father" in front of your child, or, alternatively, either overtalking about daddies or responding dismissively when your child questions you about them. Other more obvious indications are fainting, palpitations, or sweating at the mention of the "D-word." (Just kidding!) But some SMCs do find it very difficult to come to terms with this issue and cannot settle it for a long, long time. Fortunately, you have at least a couple of years after your child is born to try to work on how you feel before having to explain the situation to him.

A Child's Need to Maintain a Positive Image of His Father

If you knew your child's father and still have angry or negative feelings about him, in talking to your child you do have to cushion those feelings with "extra pillows." It is essential that you help your child to maintain a positive image of the person from whom she got half of her genetic endowment even though you may be disappointed in him, or even if he is on your list of most despicable human beings on this earth. He must have had some nice qualities or you wouldn't have been with him. (More about this in the section "If You Conceived with Someone You Knew," page 153.)

If the father was an unknown donor, you probably have some information about him that you can present in a positive way. "He was tall, had brown hair and eyes, and was very smart," for example. In addition, the fact that the man donated his sperm to help someone have a baby is in itself a positive description. You can help your child to feel proud that a nice man was willing to help you become a mom and have a family that otherwise you might not have been able to have.

Is the Question About a Father or a Daddy?

It is essential to any discussion of this subject that you be able to differentiate *in your own mind* (not necessarily to the child at this point) between the concept of a "daddy," which is a social role, and a "father," which is a biological one. Everyone has a father but not everyone has a dad. A dad is someone who loves, disciplines, and plays with his child, and usually lives with him. A father is a man whose sperm helped create a child.

So, to lay the groundwork for future discussions, when your child first asks about "daddy," keep in mind that at the beginning stage (around age two or three) she is probably not asking about her biological father but more likely about one of those people she's seen at a friend's house. An SMC once told me that she was feeling terrible because when she and her two-year-old daughter had recently visited married friends who had a child around the same age, her daughter ran after the father calling, "Daddy, daddy, daddy!" She felt sure that already her child was missing a daddy. I asked what else she would have expected her daughter to call him. She most likely heard her little friend calling him "Daddy" and assumed that was his name—not "Sam," not "Larry," but "Daddy." We have to be so careful not to read things into our children's behavior and comments that may not necessarily be there.

Young toddlers are quite concrete in their thinking and are primarily trying to understand what they see around them. The more complex and abstract questions do not occur to a child until somewhat later on, usually between four and five, and at that point you can talk with your child in a somewhat more advanced way and can include information about the biology of conception and the role of a father in your child's conception. This information will help make it clearer to the child that he, like all children, had a father but does not have a dad in his family.

WHAT IS A FAMILY?

How do you define a family and how do you want your child to define it? Do you feel comfortable saying that there are all kinds of families? How about saying that some children have two parents, a mom and a dad, and some have one parent, a mom or a dad? Or saying that some families have one parent in the home and some have two? Maybe even that a family is people who live together and love one another? If you give any of these possible responses you will be presenting a view of the world and society that is different from the traditional view with which you probably grew up. The times have changed and you have to be careful not to burden your child with outdated concepts that he will then have to unlearn, such as the traditional definition of a family as being a mother and father who are married and then have children.

Until fairly recently in our society, a family was defined only in one way: as a mom and dad who have children and stay together until they die. The great majority of families used to fit that description until the divorce rate hit record highs in the eighties. As we know from the census figures I cited earlier, today there are actually far more nontraditional than traditional families, and families with stepparents, single-parent families, lesbian and gay couples, blended families, and unmarried heterosexual couples are now commonly considered families. Are *you* willing to broaden the concept of "family"? For the benefit of your child as well as yourself, you need to define it in the broadest possible way. It is helpful to give your kind of family a name the child can use in conversation by saying something like, "There are all different kinds of families and our kind is called a single-mother family," or whatever label you feel communicates the situation best.

Be aware that whatever you tell your child is likely to be raised by him again and again, often in a very loud voice in a public place. Accordingly, you should be sure that what you have told him is the same as what you have told others and feel comfortable with them knowing. You also need to be prepared to hear your child announce various intimate details about your life in front of either total strangers or people close to you. It certainly can be embarrassing, and people will likely stare at you both, but remember that the person whose feelings you really care about is your child, not the person behind you in the ticket line at the movies.

You need to be able to address the subject with your child in as matter-of-fact a way as possible wherever and whenever the subject arises. One of our SMC members told me that she wanted to disappear right into the ground one day when her daughter, age three and a half, proudly told everyone in the supermarket line, "My father was a 'semination donor!" But instead, she smiled proudly at her daughter and said, "That's right!" It is at these unplanned, spontaneous moments that you will find out just how comfortable you are with the fact that your family is not a traditional one. And be aware that your child will also note how comfortable (or uncomfortable) you are.

PRACTICE ANSWERING THE DADDY QUESTIONS

Although the specific questions may change at different stages and developmental levels, the one most important thing at all stages, in my opinion, is *how* you answer the questions. If you respond to them in a way that is different from the way you usually answer questions, your child will notice that and wonder about it. It is important to try to become sufficiently comfortable with the daddy issue that you can actually answer those questions in very much the same way you would answer any other important and emotionally charged (but not devastating) question!

Ask yourself how you feel when you imagine your child asking the question "Do I have a daddy?" Do you sense a little bit (or a lot) of tension in yourself? Now ask yourself what that is about. Is it in response to some discomfort within yourself about the answer that comes to mind? And what answer does come to mind? The words you find yourself using in your own imaginary dialogue are often clues to how you feel. Sometimes you may think you feel just fine about the situation, but then hear yourself thinking about it and telling yourself, "Lots of children have it worse," or "I did the best I could." Of course there is nothing wrong with thinking those things, and in fact they are true statements, but they may indicate that you are still feeling guilty and are trying to either reassure yourself about your decision or dissuade yourself from the feeling that you did something wrong. Reassurance may help, but if it doesn't you may have to look a little deeper into your feelings and try to understand why you are not able to resolve the matter within yourself. A few sessions early on with a sensitive counselor or therapist may be a wise investment and prevent the need for much more counseling for you and also for your child at a later date when things have gotten more complex.

A good next step is to practice saying your thoughts out loud when your child is not around. It is amazing how sometimes we are perfectly relaxed when saying something in our minds but find it quite a different matter when we try to say it out loud. You may find yourself stumbling over certain words such as "daddy" or "sperm donor," and you may be surprised to hear your tone of voice. You may find that you sound a bit defensive or tense even though you felt quite sure that you were perfectly comfortable about the subject. If you give yourself some opportunities to practice saying these thoughts out loud, when the time comes and you are trying to help your child with them you will be much more relaxed.

Talking About It in Front of Your Child

In addition to practicing some dialogues in your own mind and aloud, another technique many SMCs have found helpful is to discuss the matter in front of your child but without the child having to actively participate in the conversation. When you are visiting or talking on the phone with a friend or relative there are many opportunities for your child to overhear you talking about and giving answers to some of the daddy questions even before she has ever asked them. It also gives your child a chance to sense your attitude about the subject and to see that you are comfortable with it and willing to talk about it. You'd be surprised how sensitive even very little kids can be about what might upset their moms and how they sometimes won't raise a subject if they believe their parent will be upset by it.

Of course, if you try this technique you will have to keep in mind that your child is listening to every word you say, so be sure that you only say what she can handle hearing. If you are talking about donor insemination, for example, it is fine to talk about it in a general, matter-of-fact way, but don't go into any intimate details of medical procedures, which might alarm a child. If you are angry with the child's father, this would *not* be the time to rant and rave about his lack of maturity or inability to commit, but it would be a good time to mention that you think your child may have gotten her artistic talent or her athletic talent (or whatever) from her father, describe some of your good times together, or mention some of the qualities you liked about him. This will help your child have and maintain a positive image of her father, who is, don't forget, the source of 50 percent of her genetic heritage.

One thing that is definitely *not* helpful is to talk about the daddy subject in front of your child in a secretive way. Sometimes if you have strong feelings about the situation it is tempting to go into it while talking with a friend, but if your child is at all able to hear you he may sense that you are talking about something relevant to him, and your secretiveness will be upsetting. Also, you really cannot be sure that he is not able to hear you, at least partially, even though you think you are being very quiet. When mothers whisper, children often manage to somehow develop superior hearing while pretending not to hear a word. One day I was speaking on the phone very quietly to a friend about something, certain that my son, then six, could not hear. After about ten minutes he yelled from another room, "Could you speak a bit louder, Mom? I had a little trouble hearing the last couple of sentences." He had heard nearly every word!

Such devices as spelling the word "father" or the man's name in conversation do not work for very long, as children seem to have an uncanny ability to figure out that kind of thing. Saying something is "private" or "for grown-ups only" is sometimes necessary, but if the conversation is about her father, a subject in which the child would be especially interested, it is not fair to her to know that she is being excluded from such a discussion—any child would resent it.

When a child is adopted, parents are advised to use the term "adopted" in front of the child from the earliest stages so that the language becomes a part of the child's world even before he can speak or understand words. Similarly, if you have conceived with donor insemination you may also want to use the terms "insemination" and "donor" and "sperm bank" at home and around friends and relatives as early as possible so your child (and the adults) can get used to hearing the words.

You can talk about donor insemination in the child's presence without explanation until such time as the child asks for a definition. Keep in mind that whatever terms you use will be the ones that your child uses later on, so choose your words carefully. "Donor insemination" is the generally preferred term, but "artificial insemination" or just "insemination" are also frequently used. The reason that some SMCs prefer "donor insemination" to "artificial insemination" is because donor insemination carries within it the reference to the donor and thereby leads logically to you and your child talking about the donor in discussion, while the term "artificial" has a more detached medical or technological feeling to it. And, as I heard one SMC say at a workshop, "There's nothing artificial about *my* child!"

Make a Picture Book About an SMC Family

Many SMCs make their own picture books about a child who lives in an SMC family and read them to the child from the earliest possible time. I think it is a good idea to change the names of the characters to allow your child to have a little distance from the story in the book, but make the story identical to your particular situation. You can draw pictures to illustrate it or clip out pictures from magazines.

If you conceived by donor insemination, the story might tell how a woman (you, but with a different name) was yearning for a child, how she tried to find a man who also wanted a child to be her husband, that she was unable to find such a man, and so she decided to go to a doctor who helps women who do not have husbands become single mothers. Or, similarly, you can tell the story of your conception with a man who was not able to be a good father for whatever were his reasons or of your quest to find a child to adopt. You can make the story as detailed or as simple as you like, since your child will not be able to read the book by himself initially. When you read the story to him you can leave out whatever portions you feel he is not yet able to comprehend, either until he is able to understand them or until he learns to read.

By turning your personal story into just another one of the many stories your child knows well after hundreds of repetitions, you are allowing him to integrate many of the concepts without having to put himself into the picture. At some point, if your child starts to recognize the similarities to your family, you can confirm that he is right. When a child catches on and asks you directly if that is his story, that can be a nice way to open up the whole subject. Mothers who have used their own storybooks report that the children treasure them and love to hear them read over and over again.

With these kinds of preparations, the groundwork will be laid for toddler years when the questions usually begin.

A TODDLER'S FIRST QUESTIONS

Keep It Simple
When a young toddler (around two or three, depending upon the child) is seeking a simple answer to a factual question, the simpler the answer the better. Unless you sense there is more to the question than a request for information or clarification, try not to complicate the matter. If you are an SMC, the real answer to the question "Do I have a daddy?" at the earliest stages is "No, our family doesn't have a dad." By phrasing the answer in the context of "our family" you are doing several helpful things at once. First, you are sharing the situation with the child rather than focusing it on her. It is a little harsher to say, "You don't have a daddy," than to say, "*We* don't have a daddy in our family." Second, when you say something about "our family" you are suggesting that other families may be

different and, implicitly, that there are *many* different kinds of families. And last, you are saying that you and your child are a family. Some people may say that a family by definition has to have two parents, but you have to be clear that a single-parent family is a family.

Resolve Your Own Feelings

If you find it is very difficult for you to imagine yourself saying something clear and simple in response to these early questions, you may, as mentioned before, still have to resolve some of your own issues about choosing to become a single mother. Some SMCs feel guilty that they are depriving the child of the advantages of two loving parents and that they are therefore at best not giving the child all they should and at worst inflicting pain on the child. No parent can help but want to give her child as much as possible, and an SMC is clearly not giving her child two parents, at least not at the outset of the child's life. But there is no clinical evidence that not having two parents from the start in and of itself causes harm or pain to a child. And keep in mind the study I mentioned earlier, which demonstrates that children raised from the outset with a never-married mother, when evaluated in adolescence, are doing better academically and have a better emotional adjustment than children from divorced or remarried stepfamilies.[*]

If you feel guilty at first, you need to get beyond that stage and realize that a less than ideal situation is not necessarily synonymous with a bad situation. A child who feels wanted, respected, and loved by even one parent and who did not have to undergo the disruption of a divorce will be far luckier than many children in two-parent families.

[*]Demo and Acock. "Family Structure and Adolescent Behavior."

Unresolved guilt feelings usually create problems, especially if you attempt to compensate for the missing parent by trying to be a supermom. Pressuring your child to be some kind of superkid in order to show the world that he can grow up just fine with only one parent, or showering him with material possessions or exaggerated affection to make up for the lack of a dad, are other signs of problematic attempts to cope with guilty feelings. Usually a child senses that you are trying to compensate for something when you do these things, and you end up creating a whole other set of problems as your child realizes he can manipulate you because of your guilt feelings. It puts the child in the position of having a kind of power over you, and no child benefits from feeling stronger than his parent.

Another common problem for an SMC is confusing her feelings about her own father with her child's feelings about *her* father. If, for instance, you never felt as close to your dad as you would have liked, or if he died or left you when you were a child, then you have suffered a loss and may be left with hurt or angry feelings or some unresolved yearnings. You may be (incorrectly) assuming that your child will feel as you do, or did, when in fact your child has *not* lost or been hurt by a parent as you were. In order to experience the loss of something, we need to have had it first, and since our children never had a dad, they cannot have lost one. They may yearn for one, wish they had one, or not, but they have not lost their dad. Similarly, if you had a wonderfully close relationship with your dad, you may wish that you could have given that to your child and assume that your child will miss having it as you feel you would have missed having it—but again, your child is most likely not in the same situation as you were.

A Little Cushioning but Not Too Much

When your child asks at this early stage about his dad, you might feel that you should try to soften or cushion the impact of the answer, as in, "No, but you have a grandpa and a grandma and four cousins and six uncles and seven aunts." "No, but" may soften the blow but it also may cause some confusion. After all, when your child asks if you have a sleeping bag or a piano or whatever, you usually would answer with a simple "No" or perhaps a "No, why do you ask?" but you would not say, "No, but we have a radio and a typewriter and a refrigerator."

The "No, but" answer can be useful at a slightly later stage when the child may be asking for reassurance, needing to know that he is loved by more people than just you. However, at this age (around two) the impact usually does not need to be softened since the toddler often has little or no idea what a daddy really is, much less an understanding of the profound emotional implications that some of us associate with having or not having one. If he doesn't know what a dad really is, why would it necessarily be a blow to learn that he doesn't have one? In fact, he most likely has looked around the house and has already realized that there is no daddy-type person around and is merely checking with you to validate what he has already figured out. Kids do that a lot.

THREE- AND FOUR-YEAR-OLDS' QUESTIONS

Although the three- to four-year-old is still pretty concrete in his thinking, he is capable of a little more depth and also capable of expressing himself a bit more than the very young toddler. You may be surprised at the real kinds of conversations you can have at this age, although still on a very simple level.

Check Out What the Child Thinks Before Answering

It is often very, very useful to ask a child what he thinks is the answer to his own question rather than leaping in to answer too quickly. Often a child has an answer in mind when asking the question, and that answer is important for you to know. The imagined answer is often a misconception or distortion of the situation, and if you don't hear what it is you cannot correct it. Keep in mind that, even if you do correct it, your child may not be able to take in the correction because he is still caught up with whatever fantasy he might have had. For example, your child may ask where his dad is, and when you ask where he thinks he is, the child may reply, "He's dead, right?" You may say very clearly that he is not dead (if that is the case) but you may still hear your child telling others or repeating to you that his dad is dead even after you have corrected that statement. Why is that?

For young children, their inner reality (fantasy or imagination) is stronger than outer reality for a fairly long time, generally until after age five or six. It may be upsetting for you to hear your child's distortions of reality, but keep in mind that understanding the realities of life is part of an ongoing developmental process for all children that improves as they mature. When this happens with a school-age or older child, he may have heard what you said and possibly even have accepted it, but may be giving what he thinks is the expected answer—perhaps something he has heard someone else say in another situation.

How Was the Question Asked?

If the question seems to be laden with more emotion than just a simple request for clarification of the facts, perhaps your child has seen or heard someone else react with strong emotion upon learning about your family's not having a dad. Remember, you may be relatively comfortable with the situation, especially after having worked on your own feelings, but your child also hears others—relatives and other children, for instance—talking about it and may sense that something about it is upsetting to them. If that is the case, you need to reassure her that there are all kinds of families and that your family is called a single-parent family. You might want to add some kind of reassuring phrase indicating that you think your family is a wonderful family. If your child is a little older and can understand a bit more, you can explain also that grandma and grandpa or cousins Joey and Mary are more accustomed to two-parent families.

Is There an Innate Longing for a Dad?

There is some controversy among experts in the child development field as to whether or not there is an innate longing for a dad in all children, regardless of whether or not the child has ever known his or her dad. I have observed many, many SMC children all across the country over the past twelve years and I have found that such a longing is not necessarily innate. I have heard some SMC children express a wish that they had a dad, but when it has been expressed in a particularly strong way, I have found that there were certain specific life circumstances in those cases—for example, the child might have suffered significant early loss (as in the death of a loved grandparent) or the child might have had particularly difficult early years, perhaps spending time in several different foster homes prior to an adoption plan being made. Another circumstance that seems to create strong desires for a dad is when a child does not feel he is getting enough contact and/or time with his one parent, the mother, or when the mother has recently stopped seeing a boyfriend to whom the child had become attached.

The typical yearning for a dad is fairly straightforward, usually expressed briefly and then dropped as the toddler goes on to other things. It is nice to acknowledge it and appreciate the child's feelings ("Yes, I understand that you would like to have a dad in our family") or ask the child more about it ("Why would you like to have a dad?"), but it is not necessary to get into a major discussion unless you sense that it is more than a casual passing comment. If your child is upset or confused, you should definitely ask him what he thinks about the situation or what he thinks it would be like if you had a dad in the family. It may open up an opportunity to get to know what he feels and to clarify his feelings a little.

Keep in mind that if a baby or toddler has suffered severe early deprivation, such as having lived in an abusive or neglectful home, she may always suffer from some degree of deprivation and crave an above-average degree of attention and love that is beyond the capabilities of any one (and often even two) parent(s) to satisfy. She may be insistent about asking you to find her a dad, symbolically placing the yearning for more love on the missing dad.

Similarly, it may be difficult for a child who has an overly busy mother to admit (even to herself) that her mother isn't giving her enough attention or that she is angry at or wants more from her. This is especially true if she senses that her mother is overwhelmed or feeling stretched to her limit. In such cases, it may be easier for the child to express a wish for an additional parent than to risk criticizing and upsetting an already stressed parent. Many children are exquisitely sensitive to their parents' emotional states and are particularly aware of when a parent, in this case the mother, is at her emotional limit. Rather than complain that one parent isn't giving them enough, the child begs for a second parent—a dad.

Living in a one-parent family gives the child an easy target on which to blame all his troubles. Be careful that you don't fall victim to the refrain, "If I had a dad. . . ." When my son once suggested to me that if our family had a dad he could have every single Nintendo game that he wanted, I was able to correct that assumption simply by pointing out to him that many of his friends had dads in their families but they still did not have every game they wanted. (And, for that matter, I added, if I had all the money in the world, I still would not buy him every single Nintendo or any other game.)

Many SMCs have observed that when their baby or toddler is around a man the child reacts in startlingly different ways toward him than she does with her mom or other women. Some kids become almost awestricken, staring at the man as if he were a prince on a white horse. Others become hyped up, obviously excited and stimulated in a different way than they are with women. These are reactions that are to be expected and have to do with the different ways children respond to men and women, rather than with any innate longing. Pediatrician T. Berry Brazelton of Harvard has documented how even very new babies will respond differently to the sound of their mother's voice and their father's voice and also to each of their presences in the room. Babies become excited and stimulated by their dad's voice or presence while being soothed and reassured by their mother's.

Let Your Child Express His Feelings About Not Having a Dad
How far have you come in resolving whatever discomfort or guilt you had about not providing a dad for your child? In the balance, as mentioned earlier, if your child senses that *you* feel all right about being a single-parent family without a dad, that has more impact in the long run than the reactions of others. Nevertheless, it is to be expected that at times your child may be confused, angry, or upset about it, and it is important to let him experience and express his feelings, even if they differ from yours, while at the same time maintaining your own equilibrium. Listening and letting him know that you understand how he feels is the best thing you can do at such a time, and your child will appreciate your doing so.

THERE ARE NO RIGHT ANSWERS

Whenever I do workshops about the daddy issues I am often asked for the "right answers" to the children's questions about their dads. In fact, I have come to the conclusion that there are no right answers. The best way you can help your child come to terms with this subject is to be open to hearing what your child is really asking and be able to listen and respond to his concerns in an empathic and interested way. I often hear anecdotes about how a mother has prepared for the day that her child asks about his dad and has finally settled on an answer that she feels will be the most helpful, only to find that the question her child asks is not one that even comes close to fitting that particular answer!

Empathic Responses Are Important
Empathic responses are ones that, in essence, communicate that you understand what the other person is feeling. Although you may initially think it's counterproductive, in fact it is nice to let your child know that you too sometimes wish there were

a dad around. In saying that, you are helping your child feel supported and understood and not so alone in that feeling. Try, when possible, to talk about the daddy subject at relaxed, cozy moments when you can listen and respond comfortably and when you can help your child express whatever she may be feeling. Don't underestimate the value of saying things like "I understand how you feel," or "I can imagine that it might be confusing for you." In difficult times those words are sometimes the greatest comfort that we can offer anyone, and if they are combined with a hug and some real compassion, they are worth more than all the "right" answers in the world.

Answer the Question That Is Asked and Stop There

Of course the way you respond also has to do with the question that is asked. The generally accepted advice for parents to answer only the question that is asked is very applicable to this situation. You probably know the age-old anecdote about the little girl who asks her mom where she comes from. Her mom takes a deep breath, reminds herself that she has known for years that someday this difficult question would be asked, and goes into a detailed description of sperm, eggs, and other matters about conception. Much to her surprise, she is interrupted by her daughter, who says, "No, Mom. I mean my friend Lisa comes from Ohio. Where do *I* come from?" So when your child asks you a question about his father, for instance, he may be asking a concrete question as was the little girl in the preceding anecdote, and you should find out exactly what he wants to know before launching into a complex discussion about donor insemination or alternative kinds of families. He may simply want to know his father's name or his whereabouts, and when you give him that information he may well be satisfied until the next question occurs to him.

FIVE- AND SIX-YEAR-OLDS' QUESTIONS

With a child of five or six who has already gotten past the stage where she is only able to grasp concrete facts, the level of questioning becomes more abstract and therefore more challenging for you to deal with than it was earlier. By this time she will have seen enough families with dads to have a working idea of what a dad is, and if the ones she has seen are nice, she may well wish that your family had one. She may have asked you to get one or in some other way let you know that she would like to have one around. Unless you hear some real indication that there is intense emotion behind this, you can respond to it as you would to any other wish. You might ask the child to tell you a little about what kind of dad she would like and/or why she would like one. And you might say, "Yes, it would be nice," or "I would like that too."

Listen carefully. It is definitely helpful to let your child express any longings and to be appreciative of them. As I mentioned in "Is There an Innate Longing for a Dad?" on page 139, sometimes your child may be wanting more time or attention from you, but instead of being that direct she may put it in terms of wanting a second parent. Asking why may help clarify this. She may say that if she had a dad he would play with her for hours and hours, have endless patience, and read her hundreds of stories, or something similar. Ask yourself if you have been especially busy or preoccupied recently. If so, you might want to acknowledge this to your child and let her know that you understand how she feels and that you will try to figure out some ways to give her more time or attention or to try to be home more.

What Is the Emotional Tone of the Question?

If there is a lot of emotion in the question, you need to determine what this reaction is about and, if possible, where it came from. Perhaps the reason has to do with an encounter with another child. Sometimes when an SMC child tells a child from a two-parent family that he doesn't have a dad, the other child may be shocked or frightened, especially if the other child has a dad to whom he is very attached. The response would probably be similar if you or anyone else were told that someone had no arm or leg—namely, "What happened to it?" When your child registers the other child's shock and then comes to you with the same question, you may hear some anxiety or fearfulness in the question that wasn't there before.

It is important to understand that children usually assume until proven otherwise that everyone is just like them. Therefore, if a child from a two-parent family learns that your family doesn't have a daddy, she will assume that, like her, your child had a dad and that something happened to him. She may get anxious, fearing that if something happened to the dad in your family, then maybe something equally terrible could happen to the dad in her family. Or the children may have had a conflict during play and the other child may be using the fact that she has two parents and your child has only one to show her superiority. This is really just a variation on the kinds of things children say to one another in anger all the time, such as, "My mom is smarter than your mom," or "Our TV is bigger than your TV!"

If the other child's reactions upset or worry your child, he will probably come to you with confusion and some big questions, spoken or unspoken, such as "Did my daddy die?" or "Did he go away?" This is a situation when reassurance and soothing are suitable and helpful. You want to assure your child (and, if appropriate and possible, the other child, too) that your family did not suffer some mysterious or devastating loss or casualty. First, try to remember to ask your child what he thinks happened to his dad, so you can get some idea of what fantasies he is having. After that is clarified, you can correct any misinformation and explain that there are all kinds of different families in the world, and that some families have dads in them and others do not. It may help to tell them the name of your kind of family. "We live in a single-parent family, which means there is one parent. Judy lives in a two-parent family, and they have two parents," you might say. Another way to put it is "Some children live with one parent and some live with two." Ideally, if you know other single-parent families, you can remind your child of his other friends who live in the same kind of family as yours.

A Young Child's Views of the World

In the earliest years a child sees the world almost entirely through the eyes of her parent(s). Your child will take what you say as the truth and not really have her own ideas or opinions for many years to come. Her answer to the question of what to say about "Daddy" thus will be essentially whatever you see as the truth, and will reflect a combination of both the words you say and the tone in which you say them.

Even after your child understands that she lives in a single-parent family, do not assume that she also understands the full implications of the concept "single." In our culture "single" means that you are the sole parent in the home and/or that you are not married. But that is not necessarily what it means to a child. Keep in mind that three- or four-year-olds, and even many older children, haven't the remotest understanding of the real meaning of the concepts of marriage and divorce and don't necessarily associate the word "single" with being unmarried but are more likely to connect it with the concept of "one," as in having one child. My own son at age nine told me that he always assumed that "single parent" meant the parent had only one child!

Young children often equate marriage with having babies. Parents sometimes realize that when they hear their child telling a friend, "My parents got married and had me, then they got married and had my sister, and now they got married again and I'm getting a new baby brother or sister in two weeks." Sometimes children have the facts about the birds and the bees but cannot fathom why anyone would have sex except to conceive a baby. Alex, a six-year-old child of an SMC, was astonished one day to hear his mother discussing the reasons she had never married. "What??!!" Alex interrupted. "You mean you were never married to my father? Then how did you have me?" His mother, who had conceived with a known donor, had never realized that Alex just assumed that at some point his mother and father had to have been married. At a later point, discussing the same general subject again, Alex asked his mom if she had ever had sex other than with his father. His mom replied, "Well, yes, I did, Alex." "Oh, my God," he responded in horror, "you had sex *twice*???"

While your words will gradually change with your child's developmental level and ability to understand more complex concepts, I can't stress too strongly that your tone of voice and way of responding will always be noticed and have an impact far greater than the words themselves. If you usually answer questions in a casual way but then answer the first daddy question in a markedly formal or elaborate way, your child will note that and wonder why. Or if you are usually chatty in answering questions and answer this one in a monosyllabic or tense way, that will also be noticed.

DIFFERENTIATING BETWEEN A FATHER AND A DAD

Unlike a younger child, your five- to six-year-old is ready to understand the notion of biological conception. At this point, you can start to help him differentiate between a father and a dad. It is helpful to explain that everyone has a father whose seed or sperm helped make him, but not everyone has a dad who lives with him. You can discuss this in terms of humans or animals, whichever you feel more comfortable with. It is very easy to talk about it at this early stage because it is not much more astonishing or embarrassing to the child than most of the other amazing things in life that he is learning about.

As a rule, children are quite matter-of-fact about sexual information until much later in their development. You may have to put up with your child announcing to total strangers that he has a penis or she has a vagina, but if you can keep your sense of humor about it, you will survive those embarrassing moments. I will never forget what happened when I visited my cousin's home with my mother to see my cousin's five-year-old daughter, Katie. Katie beamed at my then sixty-seven-year-old mother and greeted her with, "You are a lady and you have a 'gina. I have a 'gina too and so does my mom, but you know what? My daddy has a penis!" I tried very hard to keep a straight face as my mother struggled to figure out how to respond to this startling declaration.

Private Versus Secret

Children cannot keep secrets. It is developmentally impossible in the early years, and it is unfair to expect a child to be able to keep a secret at a young age or to burden a child by asking her to try to keep something secret. This presents you with a dilemma, in that you may not want the world to know the intimate details of your life, such as how you conceived your child, but neither do you want to convey that it is a big secret or something that should be hidden. Most children assume that if something is a secret, that means it is somehow shameful or bad, so you will want to talk about information being "private" rather than secret. You need to convey to her that the facts about her origins are private, and that they are not something to discuss with just anyone, but that it is *definitely* okay to discuss them with close friends or family. A five-year-old, who may understand your words when you say some things are private, and may even nod when you ask if she understands, still cannot be expected to have the self-containment to keep any information to herself until she is at least seven or eight. Even then, there may be occasional slips.

It is important to gently encourage your child to maintain some privacy while not conveying any pressure on her to do so. It is similar to helping a child understand that going to the bathroom is an okay thing to do, but it is something that is usually talked about and done only in private. Frequent gentle reminders are usually necessary until the child remembers it on her own.

DEALING WITH THE DADDY QUESTION AT SCHOOL

If you have a choice, it is helpful to choose a school that is supportive of your being an SMC. You will find that some schools are more progressive than others. Before you enroll your child, ask the director or principal (or whomever you can get an interview with) how they present the concept of "family" to the children and whether or not they discuss single-parent families. Ask if there are any other SMCs' children attending the school and see if you can arrange to speak with some of them. Try to determine whether the administrator of the school has an unbiased attitude, and whether he or she seems to be comfortable with you as an SMC. If the administrators are moralistic or judgmental you might do better with another school.

Or, if you have no good choices, you might have to show the school personnel by your example that a single mother can be a terrific mom. It may be possible to find out what prejudices or misunderstandings they have (they might think your child was rejected or abandoned by his father, or believe that all single mothers by choice are narcissistic, selfish yuppies who regard their children as little toys) or it may not, but you can show them who *you* are as opposed to their stereotypes. As they get to know you and see how much you care about your child, they may be able to move beyond their preconceptions toward a more contemporary view of the world and be more accepting of alternative families.

Of course, regardless of how positive an administrator may be, there is no guarantee of what the individual teachers may think. Some will probably be more comfortable with alternative families than others. If you can sit in on a class and meet a few teachers, that is helpful, but there will always be personnel changes. You probably will have to be prepared to work with at least some of the teachers to foster their understanding of your situation and discuss how they can best be helpful to your child.

One of my son's nursery school teachers was initially very disapproving of SMCs, although the school director was quite positive about them. I went out of my way to talk to this teacher and let her get to know us. I told her that I shared her concerns about what effect my son's not having a dad might be having on him. I added that I was interested in knowing if my son asked any questions or expressed any feelings about not having a dad. After we had talked a few times she was open-minded enough to be able to realize that she had been carrying around an unfair prejudice and honest enough to admit it. But she didn't stop there.

One day she decided to address this issue head-on with her class of four-year-olds. She read them a book about a chipmunk family and then opened up the discussion to include human families. "Does everyone get married?" she asked them. Of course, being four, they thought that was true, and so she gently told them that some people do get married and others don't. She then asked them if only married people could have babies and they were quite sure that this was so. Again, she gently told them that some people who have babies are not married and that some married people do not have babies. She explained that it is best to have a baby when you are mature enough to take care of it and that young people are better off not having babies until then, but if you are mature, she said, you can raise a child well if you are married or not.

I was thrilled at her taking what I felt was a courageous position and expected that she was going to be hearing from some irate parents. (She had, of course, cleared this lesson with the school director.) As far as I know there were no complaints from any of the parents. It may be that telling the children about single parenthood at such an early age is easier than it is later, as is talking about sex, since it is not any more remarkable than many other things they are learning. In fact, the children may not have even mentioned it to their parents. (A side note: children at this age hardly ever tell their parents anything about what happened at school. When I used to ask my son what he did at nursery school, the standard answer was, "We had snack." On a particularly chatty day he would reply, "We had snack and played in the playground.")

With an older child, some of the teachers in your child's school will have no idea what kind of family she comes from and will not necessarily care as much as does a nursery school teacher. There is always the possibility that a teacher's prejudices or lack of sensitivity will come through and you may have to help your child come to terms with a teacher who refers to children of unmarried parents as "bastards" or as "illegitimate" children. Should such a thing happen, a visit to the school administrator is called for as quickly as possible both to correct and to educate the teacher and also so that your child's classmates do not get the idea that this is an acceptable way to describe a person. There is nothing illegitimate about any children—they are all very legitimate little beings, and as for the word "bastard," that simply does not belong in the mouth of any teacher. Another common problem is that teachers or other school personnel sometimes refer to our children as coming from "broken" homes or "broken" families. There is nothing broken about our families or homes; they are loving, intact, though small families. Do not hesitate to help educate the school personnel about these terms.

At this point we have to discuss the daddy issue from two different perspectives—one for those who conceived with someone they knew and the other for those who conceived with an unknown donor. Both raise issues you will want to understand so you can best help your child to deal with them.

IF YOU CONCEIVED WITH SOMEONE YOU KNEW

When you actually knew or know the father, the crucial matters in discussing the daddy questions are your current relationship with and your feelings about the father today, particularly whether or not you are angry with him, and also whether or not he knows about the child's existence. Was he someone whom you knew and loved for a long time and who is more like an ex-husband than just a biological father? Or was he someone you knew casually and minimally? Were you clear that you wanted him just to father a child for you, or did you hope for an ongoing relationship with him and were disappointed? Do you have only resentful or upsetting feelings when you think about him, or are your feelings more mixed? Can you maintain some appreciation of his biological contribution to your child's conception? Is he still in your life and will he be in the child's life in the future? Do you feel you have to protect him in some way (as in the case of a married man who may have a family of his own that does not know about your family)? And have you thought about whether or not you will want to help your child someday if he wants to find and meet his father?

Your feelings about these various aspects of the situation will very probably be stirred up by whatever your child may ask you and will come across in your response. To reiterate, it is important to try (if you possibly can) to work out whatever anger and/or disappointments you have with the biological father before your child is old enough to start asking questions. That way, when the questions start, you can respond in a way that is based on the child's needs rather than your own, and you can be relatively neutral, and ideally even positive, rather than blame or attack the father because you are still angry with him.

I cannot stress strongly enough how important it is not to talk about the father in a negative or critical way and to help your child maintain a positive image of him. You will need to be able to come up with a picture of this man in your own mind that is tilted toward the positive side of reality. No one is perfect, and you shouldn't try to present him as perfect either, but you need to try to mention anything positive about the man that you can and deemphasize the negative. You will ultimately need to be able to describe him as, for example, a man who had a great sense of humor, a talent for cooking, and a nice sense of adventure—and *not* mention that he did some things that hurt you very deeply (or that he is someone with whom you would not want to have a serious relationship because he took drugs, or whatever the case may be). You cannot present him as bad or even deeply flawed without causing your child to fear that if his father is like that, he must in some way also be like that. If you cannot get yourself to that point, counseling or therapy, as mentioned earlier, can be a real help. Once your child nears adulthood you can be more honest.

If your child asks why his father is not around, remember the point I made earlier: *don't forget to ask the child what he thinks.* That is more important than any answer you can give. Many SMCs have been shocked by the answers they got when they asked their children what they thought. Some children thought that their dads were among the homeless people on the street in their city. Others thought that their fathers were in jail or dead. After you have learned what your child thinks, you can clarify whatever confusion there may be. Then you can explain the reality: that either you or he felt it would be best if you stopped seeing one another, if that was the case, or that you and he lost touch, or whatever, without placing blame on anyone.

You need to think about what you will say if your child wants to meet her father at some point. If you know his whereabouts, would you be willing to help your child get in touch with and meet him, and if so, at what age? If you do not know where he is, you may still be able to locate him if it is important to your child. I think it is best to wait until the child is eighteen, as is the practice with those sperm donors who agree to be contacted by the children they father, or as close to that age as possible, so that your child is fairly mature and able to understand the significance of the situation. It is likely that it will be an emotional meeting, and your son or daughter will need considerable preparation. If you feel the man is so unacceptable that you never want your child to meet him, you may not even want to reveal the father's name. It is something you and your child will have to sort out between you as she approaches adulthood and becomes more able to make her own decision about this. If you have been out of contact with the man, you may want to be a go-between and make the initial contact to let him know that his child is considering asking to meet him. That way he will have a chance to think it through and will not be surprised. You may not want to let your child make the initial contact because a surprised father may be rude or nasty, and even if you try to prepare your child for that possibility, it will still be a blow. If the man refuses your preliminary request for a meeting, then you have to decide whether to try to protect your child from asking and being rejected, or whether you prefer him to have tried and faced reality and then deal with the rejection.

When the question "What is my daddy's name?" arises, it calls for different answers depending upon whether or not you are comfortable letting your child know the name. If you feel you can reveal it, you might want to respond to the question using the term "father," as in, "Your father's name is David." In that way you are both very gently correcting the child (not his *dad*, but his *father*) and also laying the groundwork for future discussions once your child can distinguish between the concepts "daddy" and "father."

Similarly, if your daughter asks where her father is, depending upon whether or not you know, you can reply accordingly. If you give her the name of the city or state in which he lives, if you know it, that may satisfy her curiosity for the time being as well as offer her a socially acceptable response to friends' questions about her dad. She can then say, "My father's name is Dave," and, perhaps, "He's in Vermont," and that may take care of the subject for that phase.

Some children come up with this sort of answer to other people's questions on their own.

Beth

Beth's daughter, Jennifer, at age seven, regularly used to answer her friends' questions about her dad's whereabouts by replying that he was in Arizona. The first time Beth overheard this response she was totally flabbergasted, as she knew the father was not in Arizona and she couldn't imagine where Jennifer had come up with that (mis)information. But, Beth noticed, this reply answered the friend's question and seemed to end the discussion, so she decided to let it be for a while. She appreciated that the response was one that worked for Jennifer with her peers, and she assumed that at some point Jennifer would ask where her father was, a question that Jennifer had not yet actually raised. Beth also reasoned that there was no real need for Jennifer, at this age, to know exactly where her father was and that the actual facts would really only matter if in the future Jennifer wanted to try and find him.

Two years later, Jennifer asked her mom where her father lived, saying, "He's in Arizona, right, Mom?" When Beth told her that was not the case, Jennifer actually argued with her, insisting that Beth had told her so! Obviously Jennifer was convinced for some reason that this was the truth. After thinking about it for a while, Jennifer came back and told her mother that she had remembered that a distant family cousin lived in Arizona, and that she might have heard that mentioned and somehow gotten it confused with her dad's whereabouts. "So," she asked Beth, "where is he?" Jennifer was amazed to learn that he was only about fifteen minutes away from their home, not the three hours' distance to Arizona!

IF YOU CONCEIVED WITH AN UNKNOWN DONOR

If you have used donor insemination to conceive, it is important that you feel relatively comfortable about others knowing that fact, since once you tell your child you can be sure that he will tell others. Remember, children cannot keep secrets. It is developmentally impossible in the early years, and it is unfair to expect a child to be able to keep a secret at a young age or to burden him by asking him to. (See the discussion of private versus secret on page 148.)

As our society is becoming increasingly comfortable with advanced medical technology, people are now somewhat less surprised to learn that you may have become pregnant by donor insemination or in vitro fertilization. In particular, the children of today rarely find this surprising at all. In fact, they are less shocked by the idea of using technology to conceive than they are at the idea of sexual intercourse—at least into their early teens. It is the adults who are more difficult to deal with, as they have lived with traditional values and methods of conception for much of their lives and are sometimes reluctant or unable to accept change. You will most likely find that explaining the donor-insemination means of conception to your child is not particularly difficult (assuming that you have worked out your feelings about it) since a child has no preconceived notions about what is "normal" or unusual. If you said that he had been conceived by rubbing two sticks together or by turning around in a circle and chanting, he would accept that equally well. So remember that what is essential is that you have worked out your feelings well enough so that you can convey this information to your child in a simple and neutral way, and then wait for his questions.

WHEN YOUR CHILD IS OLDER

The very complex issues relating to your having conceived by donor insemination will come up when your child is old enough to understand that her conception was by an unusual method and that she has significantly less information than most children have about their fathers. She may start to realize these kinds of things as she nears her teens. The big question children want answered is what their father is like, and this may be more or less of a burning issue depending upon the child. In the case of adopted children, some are very eager to learn as much as they can about their birth parents, while others just do not care as much, and this is likely also to be true of children conceived by donor insemination. (For a lovely example of a discussion between a mother and child on this subject, see the case of Laurie, p. 36.)

How much information you are able to give your child depends upon the policies of the sperm bank that you used. But no matter how much you have, your child may well want more, and you will have to help her come to terms with the fact that you only have limited information. As she gets older she will understand more about the reasons for this, and when she is first struggling with it, an empathic and interested stance on your part will be most helpful. If you have used a sperm bank that allows the child to find the donor after the child is eighteen, that information will be important so you can reassure the child that at some point she *may* be able to actually meet the person. However, there is always the possibility that the donor either changed his mind or that the sperm bank lost track of him, so you cannot really guarantee that such a meeting will take place in the future. All you can say for sure is that you will help your child to try to find the donor.

I cannot conclude this section without making one important point. A child *can* grow up and do fine without having a dad. It may at times be confusing, but it doesn't have to be devastating, particularly if you can be helpful to your child in dealing with the issue. Empathetic listening and acceptance of your child's feelings is invaluable. And expect the feelings to change at different stages and even from week to week.

6

....

SPECIAL CHILD DEVELOPMENT
ISSUES FOR CHILDREN
OF SINGLE MOTHERS BY CHOICE

Besides the obvious issue of not having a dad, there are many other aspects of child development that, if understood, can help make a parent's task of raising a happy, well-adjusted child a little easier. This is even more important for an SMC because her child has some special needs that have to be taken into consideration. Some of the most obvious and important characteristics of child development that are unique to SMCs' children are that there is no second parent to help the child emotionally separate from the intense early tie to the mother, there is no built-in male figure to love your child and with whom a son can identify, nor is there a rival in the household for the mother's attention. Lastly, there are sometimes problems about being a twosome—the intensity of the relationship between parent and child, and the balance of power that a child may feel in relation to his parent when he grows up in a one-parent family (as compared with a child who grows up with two parents).

SEPARATION ISSUES

Traditionally in our society, mothers have been seen as representing nurturing and protection in the home, while fathers represent excitement and separation from the security of home and mother. (This difference was, of course, much more clear-cut before so many women were working outside the home.) The mother's role was often described by terms like "mother hen"—she was the one who held the children back from risks, while the dad was often the one who did stimulating and challenging things with them. A woman's self-esteem and her sense of importance and usefulness were very much determined by how good a mother she was to her children. Some feminists believe that one of the reasons that a woman might have been less than eager to let her children become fully independent was because it would mean that she was out of a job. Certainly it makes sense that a mother would feel less conflict about seeing her children develop independence if she had other sources of satisfaction and self-esteem, such as a career, available to her. While it is true that if a mother is a little overprotective, her child might benefit from some extra encouragement to get out there and explore the world, there is no reason why this has to come from the father. It can be provided by any person who has a close relationship with the child.

One of the important functions that a dad performs in a two-parent family is helping the child to emotionally separate from the mother. He provides an alternative to the mom's point of view, style, and temperament, and when the mother becomes too intensely intertwined with the child, he can step in and provide a cooler option. However, this function does not necessarily have to be performed by the child's biological father. If you understand and accept that the child will need a third person to step in and take over at times, you can encourage another important person or other people to be available to do so. It is surely not healthy for a child to be raised in emotional isolation with his mother as his only source of nurturing, nor is it healthy for a mother to have her child be the only emotionally gratifying person to her. One of the greatest gifts you can give your child is to let other caring people love him or her.

THE IMPORTANCE OF A MAN IN A CHILD'S LIFE

It is very valuable for both boys and girls to have a man involved with them in some intimate way from their earliest years. Half the population is male, and being able to feel comfortable and get along with both sexes is important for all of us. The sooner your child is exposed to relationships with men the better, so he or she can grow up taking men for granted as part of the world. The man does not have to be the child's father but can be any loving, reliable man who is or would like to be a part of your life. A man is important for both boys and girls, and both will benefit from having been loved by a man as well as a woman. However, a boy needs a relationship with a man in order to have a role model for masculine identification, whereas a girl needs it for the experience of loving and being loved by a man.

THE IMPORTANCE OF A MAN IN A BOY'S LIFE

Despite my erroneous conviction prior to being a mother that almost all gender stereotypes were created rather than inborn, I saw clearly early on how much my son needed a kind of roughhousing in play, something that was totally alien to me, but which almost any man who was in the vicinity seemed to understand immediately. Men appear to love to play in this rough-and-tumble way that few women seem to enjoy, and having a man to provide that kind of play will fulfill what is apparently a deep need and also bring your son many hours of pleasure. Mothers of little girls I knew didn't find that their daughters were interested in roughhousing; their little girls loved to play with dolls and stuffed animals. When I offered my son stuffed animals to play with he would promptly fling them into a far corner of the room. So, I concluded, there seem to be some innate differences between boys and girls.

A boy also needs to have a personal experience of what men are like in order to feel comfortable with men and with being a man. It is very important for him to have a role model, a man with whom he can compare himself and against whom he can measure himself as he grows into adolescence and young manhood.

So how do you as an SMC meet this need for a role model? If you are lucky, you might already have people in your life who are obvious candidates, such as a family member (a brother or cousin, or your father, perhaps) who likes children and is willing to take on the role. Another possibility is a male friend whose children are grown or who never had children and who would be interested in being there for your child. There may be a teacher who would be available for a "big brother" kind of relationship or an older child in the neighborhood who has no younger brother but would like one. If there is no obvious person, you need to use all your creativity and determination to find someone. Think about it as essential and you will probably be able to find the person.

If you cannot find anyone through your own networking efforts, there is a national, nondenominational organization called Big Brothers that has been active in many communities for a long time and which is experienced at screening and providing men who are interested in being father figures for boys who need them. Unfortunately, they will not work with children who are below school age, and I believe that the ideal is to have this kind of relationship begin in infancy or as early as possible, but when your son is old enough they are a good resource.* Some cities also have big-brother-type organizations for boys of specific religious denominations: New York City has Jewish Big Brothers, for example, which works only with Jewish boys and men.

An Example of a Male Role Model

Susan

Susan, a thirty-seven-year-old lawyer, had talked with every man she knew while she was pregnant about the possibility of him being a male role model for the son she was expecting. One or two said they might be interested, but when she actually gave birth only one of the men visited and showed a real interest, and that was Fred.

Fred and his wife, who was an old friend of Susan's, had been

---

*One of the main reasons for their only working with older boys is because of the risk that child abuse might go unreported by a younger child. These agencies screen very carefully, but mistakes can happen.

married for twenty years and had repeatedly put off having a child until they eventually realized that they didn't really want one of their own. However, Fred thought that being the "godfather" for Susan's son, Michael, would be the perfect compromise. It offered some degree of involvement yet was without the daily responsibility and stresses that come with child rearing.

Fred started visiting Michael regularly once a week when the child was just a few months old. He would spend a few hours with Michael in the afternoon and then stay for dinner. They would play together at the local playground or at home, building with blocks and roughhousing on the floor. Fred would change Michael's diapers, feed him, and take him with him on errands during their time together. As Michael got older, they would visit museums and go to movies and sometimes just hang out. The visits were very important to Michael. He called Tuesdays "Fred day."

It was important to Susan that Michael get a sense of who Fred really was, and Fred agreed. He did not want to be a Santa Claus kind of figure who came bearing gifts and never got angry or disciplined Michael. The relationship was very real, with its ups and downs, disappointments and joys. Fred took it quite seriously. He felt pleased at the opportunity to grow that it offered him, although at times he felt the responsibility to be a burden. Michael had a rather reserved personality and didn't overtly show much affection or appreciation, and Fred very much needed to feel valued. But Fred stayed in there and kept on trying to meet Michael's needs. He extended himself in ways he had never before had to, and at times all the stretching was painful. They maintained a once-a-week schedule, plus birthdays and family holidays, for nine years.

Several years later, Fred and Michael still see one another, though less frequently than before (only six or seven times a year) as both of their lives have become busier, and there are some weekend visits with Fred and his wife in their country house. Susan reports that Michael still asks her if she thinks he will be as tall as Fred when he grows up, and debates whether or not he will choose to drive the same kind of car as Fred when he is old enough to be able to buy a car. At this point in his life, he is considering becoming an accountant like Fred. Just as with many father-and-son relationships, this one was not a perfect fit, but Michael has clearly internalized Fred and used him as a point of reference as he has been growing up. Michael has benefited from the relationship greatly, and Fred says he has too.

Like relationships with one's own father, relationships with male role models come in many different forms and styles, but I believe that children of SMCs can benefit greatly from having a consistent, dependable, caring man in their lives from the earliest possible time. He does not have to be a perfect human being, but he does have to be willing to let your child into his heart and to treat their relationship as a special and important bond.

Is an SMC's Son Going to Be Overattached to His Mother?

You may know the myth of Oedipus, the young man in ancient Greece who fell in love with and married his mother after he unknowingly killed his father, and had to suffer the punishment of blindness. Many child development professionals believe that this drama is one that is universal to all families and which every boy tries to play out in early childhood between ages three and six. This may sound a little wild to a person who has not heard of or seen evidence of the Oedipal phase in children, but most parents will tell you that little boys are fairly direct about their wish to marry mom. I once was visiting friends of mine who had a four-year-old boy and in the middle of dinner he asked his mom if he could marry her. When she said that wasn't possible since she was married already to his dad, the little boy replied, "Oh, that's okay. He could leave."

In a traditional family with a mom and a dad, the boy's wish to get rid of his father and have his mother all to himself is impossible to fulfill. His dad is clearly bigger and stronger and definitely will not let his son win in the Oedipal competition. So the little boy consoles himself by identifying with his dad and (unconsciously) assuring himself that someday he too will be big and smart and strong and successful like Dad and will marry a girl "just like the girl who married dear old Dad."

Some mental health experts have expressed concern that a boy who is raised without losing to a male parental rival in this way will have some problems with his male identification since he has no reason to give up his primary identification with and attachment to his mother. They fear he either will remain identified with her and therefore become effeminate or even homosexual, or that he may feel he has "won" his mother (from the father who is not around) and will not be able to resolve his romantic attachment to her and go on to love other women as he grows into manhood.

So what about the little boys of SMCs? How will they resolve this?

Paula

Paula, an SMC I met on a visit to one of the California chapters of our group, told me that she was a little concerned because her son Mark had recently (at age four) told her quite matter-of-factly that when he grew up he was going to have lots of babies and that she was going to be their mom. She tried to suggest tactfully that she would be very happy to be the grandmother, but she would be far too old to be the mother, and anyway, she told her son, he would be much happier with a girl closer to his own age. No, Mark insisted, she would be the mom and that was definite. I suggested that she just wait and see what happened to this scenario as he got older, and reminded her not to encourage or reinforce it in any way, by being unduly seductive, for instance, or joking around about the "plan." She understood and said she would let me know how things developed.

I got a call from her one morning about three years later. She said that the subject had been mentioned by Mark a few more times, and that each time she had repeated her earlier response, but to no avail. Mark had seemed determined. He was now seven, and she told me that the previous night he had asked her how old she would be when he was old enough to have babies, say when he was twenty-five. "Sixty-two," Paula told him. He walked away and apparently did some thinking. The next morning he came to her and asked her if she remembered that he had once said he wanted to have babies with her when he grew up. She assured him that she did indeed remember that. He then announced, "Well, forget it. I've changed my mind," and went off to play his Nintendo. End of discussion. One can read into this that he had come to the conclusion that he didn't want to have babies with a sixty-two-year-old woman, but we don't really know for sure what was going on in little Mark's mind.

I asked Paula if there had been any changes in their lives or family structure, whether or not there was a man in her life or someone whom Mark might have perceived as an unbeatable rival, and she replied that there was none of that. So we have to assume, at least from this (as well as other similar anecdotal evidence), that a boy can apparently resolve the attachment to his mom without necessarily going through a rivalry and a loss. It will be interesting to learn more about the way in which our boys re-solve this phase. We will be looking to see what their choices of mates are like and whether any generalizations can be drawn about their love lives and sexual development.

Your Attitude Toward Men

Remember that your son will notice and be affected by the way you feel about men in general, and particularly about his biological father, if he was someone you knew. He has to identify with him, since he got half of his genetic endowment from him, and if you cannot speak of him in at least a neutral or slightly positive way, it will be detrimental to your son's sense of himself as a male. If you had angry feelings toward this man and have not been able to resolve them, you will be hard-pressed to help your son identify with him in a positive way. There were undoubtedly positive qualities that he had or else you would not have gotten involved with him, right?

THE IMPORTANCE OF A MAN IN A GIRL'S LIFE

Some people think that only boys really need a man in their lives, but child development experts as well as common sense say that a man is important for both boys and girls. First of all, half of the world is male, and we need to make sure that our daughters feel comfortable with both men and women as they go out into the world. The best way to bring that about is for a girl to have a close relationship with a man from the earliest months of her life. This man need not be her biological father, nor does he have to be someone with whom you have a love relationship. Your father, an uncle, a cousin, the husband of a good friend, or any caring and responsible man you know who is able to fill that role is fine, assuming that you are sure that the person is not abusive in any way.

Second, it is very important for a little girl to have experienced being loved by a man in her early years so that she has the confidence that boys and men will find her lovable as she matures. The origins for that sense of lovableness are in her earliest experiences with the important man in her life. While this important man need not be her father or even a biological relative, it *is* necessary that the affection and respect that he feels for her be communicated consistently.

Will Our Daughters Be Able to Leave Us and Love a Man?

As with the Oedipal stage previously described for boys, there is a corresponding phase for girls between approximately three and six. At this stage a little girl is often rivalrous with her mother, vying for her father's affection and often flirting outrageously with him, only to eventually lose the competition as Dad makes it quite clear that Mom is his one true love. Little girls comfort themselves after the blow of losing to Mom by identifying with their mothers, as boys do with their fathers. They decide (unconsciously) that if they grow up and are just as pretty and talented and successful as Mom, then they can marry a man just like Dad. How can a girl go through this phase if there is no dad?

Since little girls identify with their mothers from early on and are competitive with their mothers about all sorts of things, their female identification does not come solely from the resolution of the competition with their mother for their dad. An SMC's little girl may never experience the marvelous intensity of the three- or four-year-old girl's love for her dad, but little girls can (and do) develop crushes on other men or boys who are part of their lives, only to eventually have to give them up as hopeless and go on to other more available and appropriate choices later on.

As I have said before, your own attitudes toward men will be a major influence on how your little girl views men, and she will identify with you in that aspect of her development as in so many others. Be aware of the very important role that you play in shaping her future relationships with men simply by the way you talk about them and relate to them in your daughter's presence. If you are still carrying around angry feelings toward your daughter's father, you really need to resolve them so that she is not exposed to them. It would be hurtful for her to hear that you are angry at men in general, but even more so to hear that you are angry at her own biological father, who is, after all, a part of her.

SOME CAUTIONARY NOTES ABOUT A MALE ROLE MODEL

Sad though it may be, there are some very disturbed people out there, and we cannot put our heads in the sand and pretend that it is not so. If someone wants to be your child's role model and you do not know him intimately, be sure to do a careful check on him and get character references from people who do know him well. Even if you feel that you can trust the person, it is best that you remain with him during the visits for at least the first year, in the case of a toddler, or longer with a younger baby. You can leave him alone with your child at the point at which you feel sure that he or she is comfortable with him and also is able to communicate well enough that you can get some idea of how things are going.

The scariest time to leave your child in someone else's care is during the earliest years when the child does not yet have the capacity to tell you directly if anything is upsetting him. Even after the point at which your child can talk, be aware of the behavioral signs that something may not be right, such as your child not wanting to be with the person or behaving unusually after a visit.

Eventually you will be able to find a caring, decent human being who wants to have an opportunity to enjoy a special relationship with your child, but do not let your eagerness to provide your child with a male figure blind you to the possible risks.

WHAT IF YOUR SON SAYS HE WANTS TO GROW UP TO BE A MOMMY?

I don't think I will ever forget the moment that Rachel, one of the SMCs in our group, came running over to me at a meeting insisting that she talk to me right away. She told me that on a recent evening her son Ethan, age three, had told her that he wanted to be a mommy when he grew up. "Oh, no," she had said to him, in what she hoped was a tone of voice that hid her panic, "you'll be a daddy." To her dismay, he insisted that he wanted to be a mom. What was she doing wrong, she wondered?

Knowing what kind of mother Rachel was, I was pretty sure that she was not doing anything wrong. At some point in their lives, nearly all boys want to be like their moms. After all, their mother is usually the main person in their lives and does most or all of the basic caretaking in their early years. They admire and love her. Even boys who grow up in families that have both parents go through this phase of identifying with their moms in the toddler years before going on to identify with their dads at around four or five, although they may not express it so openly as Ethan did. But since there is no "daddy" figure in the house, you may have to give your son a little help to move from his identification with you to a male identification.

WHAT IS IDENTIFICATION?

In the beginning, during infancy, your baby feels that he and you (his mother) are one person. After all, when he cried with hunger, you fed him; when he was uncomfortable with a wet diaper, you changed him. You soothed him when he was upset and met all his needs. As he develops, however, the baby becomes more and more aware that you and he are separate people, and along with that knowledge comes some distress both at the loss of what was a wonderful sense of oneness and also at the awareness that, being a separate person, you can come and go at your whim, and he cannot control you as a part of himself. In order to relieve some of this emotional pain and make the separation more tolerable, your child (unconsciously) takes on some of your characteristics and personality traits. By so doing he has part of you inside of himself where you can always be with him. This is what is meant by the term "identification." A similar process is probably familiar to anyone who has ever felt she just had to bring souvenirs home at the end of a wonderful trip—both are ways of dealing with our sadness about a time that has come to an end.

If you have a daughter, the natural process of identifying with you is not as much of an issue. In the case of a son, however, while the phase is also a natural one, you might find yourself worrying more about it. It is important for you to understand this process of identification and not to panic when your son is at this stage.

You might be concerned that taking on some of your characteristics will make your son effeminate, but that is not necessarily so. Although some people may label certain traits as feminine, they often are not innately gender-linked. Nurturing, for example, is a parental quality, not a feminine one, so when you see your son being tender and loving toward a baby or pet, you might want to praise that quality while at the same time "masculinizing" it. You might say, "You were so gentle with that baby. I can see that you're going to be a great dad someday!" It is definitely *not* helpful to discourage such behavior by criticizing him for being a "sissy." Similarly, if your son says he wants to cook "just like Mommy," after you thank him you might want to mention the many men you know, famous and not, who are great cooks. In other words, it is the way you react to and interpret these traits to your son that indicates to him that you are supportive of him and of his developing masculinity, not the traits in and of themselves.

Even though this identification with Mom is natural, you'll want to make sure that your son doesn't get stuck at this stage and that he goes on to identify with being male. A family with a dad has someone for the boy to move *toward* as he is moving away from his mom, ideally someone whom he sees that his mom loves and admires. This makes the separation process, especially for a boy, a bit less difficult. In an SMC family, since there is no second parent, you need to *actively* support and help your son as he moves away from you and establishes his male identity. He needs to move toward someone, although the person does not have to be his biological father. It would be optimal if there were a man he could move toward, but any other loving person can perform the function of helping him separate from you.

Again, I want to reiterate that not having a dad around complicates these issues, but with your help, the child will be able to cope with them.

How Do You Feel About Men?

As an SMC raising a child in a family that does not have a man in it, you need to give some thought to how your child will regard and feel about men. Men are 50 percent of the people in the world, and we want our children to be able to deal comfortably with both men and women as they grow up and go out into the world. Certainly having a male role model is helpful, as described above. Another important factor in how your child feels about men is your own attitude toward men.

Because there is no man around on a regular basis, your child does not have a built-in opportunity to see you relating to men and showing love and respect toward them. In order for your son to feel good about growing up male, he needs to know that you like and admire men and that you support his strivings to become a man. Similarly, in order for your daughter to feel at ease with and warmly toward men, she needs to see that you include men as a meaningful and gratifying part of your life. For both boys and girls it is very important that they be able to get to know and experience firsthand the love of a man in addition to your love. As an SMC you need to make sure that you are giving your child opportunities to see you express your respect and affection for men in both words and actions.

How do you convey this respect? One simple way is to be sure to speak openly of and share your feelings about men whom you admire. "Uncle Jim is such a loving man" and "Mr. Rogers is so good at talking to children" are simple and easy examples. You need to be particularly aware of the need to do this kind of thing if there are few men in your life or if you don't naturally say things like this. When you and your child are with a man whom you like, you could say complimentary things about him or directly to him. Remember that your child has no way to ascertain how you feel about men unless he sees you showing your positive feelings toward men or you tell him directly.

You may be getting tired of hearing this, but I cannot stress enough how important it is for you to make sure that you have resolved whatever residual anger you may have if you were involved with your child's father in a relationship that did not work out as you would have liked it to. These feelings are potentially very damaging to your child if they are not at least made more neutral, and optimally you will be doing yourself and your child a favor if you can move your feelings into positive territory. If you have tried to do this by yourself and have not been successful, counseling or therapy can help.

DISCIPLINING WHEN THERE IS ONLY ONE PARENT

Power Struggles, or, Who's in Charge Here?

An SMC who was having trouble disciplining her son said to me recently, "My son fights with me unrelentingly, and as if he were my equal, and sometimes I really don't have as much energy for the fight as he does. At least in a two-parent family the child *knows* he's outnumbered!"

There was a lot of talk around the time of the L.A. riots in 1992 about the fact that many of the rioters came from single-parent families. The message was explicit: children growing up without a dad are undisciplined, do not develop self-control, and are going to grow up to be looters, rioters, or worse, or so the columnists said. Although the SMC children I have gotten to know in the last thirteen years show no signs whatsoever of being future criminals, I do believe that raising a child in a one-parent family presents us with some unique challenges. On the positive side, the children tend to get a great deal of attention since we can devote a lot of energy to them without having to cope with the needs of a spouse who also requires our time and attention. Another positive aspect is that most of our children were very much wanted, and they sense their importance in our lives. However, on the down side, a family of two tends to have a more intense relationship with one another than those found in a larger family, and I think that this greater intensity necessitates that we be especially clear and consistent about our parenting approach and in setting limits with our children.

Why Do Children Need Limits?

Research on newborns tells us that they feel omnipotent, they believe that they control the world. They cannot yet differentiate between their inner world and the outside world of reality, and so when their mother soothes or feeds them they feel that *they* magically made it happen. This feeling of omnipotence, although a very heady feeling at first, is gradually challenged as the baby increasingly becomes aware of how helpless and vulnerable he really is. It takes several months until a baby can sort out that it is his parent (or other caregiver) who is taking care of his needs and not the baby himself.

At the toddler stage, as the baby becomes more separate from his mother he realizes that he cannot control her—she walks away whenever she wants to, despite his screams—and he goes through a painful stage of trying to control the world, a phase often characterized by tantrums. Why the tantrums? Faced with this terrible realization of separateness, the young child tries to take charge of the situation in the only way he knows how: by becoming a tyrant. Because he is not yet mature enough to be able to use more adult options, he tries to act like a person in charge *as understood by a toddler*—that is, like a bully, a tyrant, generally not a terrific person to be around.

It is at those times when children are trying to be in charge that we adults have to step in and relieve them of the job in the most calm, firm, and loving way possible. Of course no one is a perfect parent, and we all lose it at times, but if we act in a mature way most of the time, we will be giving our children a model of adulthood they can draw upon later as they ultimately become mature adults themselves. In the meantime they will be able to feel safe in a world that sometimes is scary and confusing for a small and fairly helpless child. In the face of the child's tantrum, we must remain calm and in control. We must show our frightened children that *we* can control ourselves and we can help them control *them*selves. That is the message we need to give them in order for them to feel safe. If you are unsure about what parenting styles are best for you, there are many parenting classes and books available. Some of my favorite books are listed in Appendix E.

SHARING LIVING SPACE

Some SMCs have found that an effective way of lessening the intensity of single parenting is to share living quarters with one or more other families. If the other family has children, that can also provide a built-in playmate for your child. This can be a terrific arrangement if the people really know one another well and have developed effective ways of problem-solving and communicating. In the best of these situations it can be like a good extended family where people help one another out and share responsibilities to make life easier for all. If an SMC has forgotten one item in her shopping, there usually will be someone around to watch the baby so she doesn't have to bundle him up all over again and take him back with her to the store. On the other hand, if the people are not compatible or have not worked out a means of dealing with the day-to-day problems that inevitably arise when people live together, it can be a tense and difficult situation. A young child can be devastated if it falls apart and the people he has gotten attached to are no longer around, so if you are considering sharing a living space, think carefully about it beforehand. If you are unsure, perhaps an intermediate step such as living very close to the others while not living in the same household would be a good way to begin. And remember, whether or not you actually live with or near another family, it is important to let other adults love and get close to your child. In times of stress, both you and your child will need and appreciate having others to turn to for support and some neutral ground.

Hillary Rodham Clinton said that it takes a village to raise a child. I'd say it takes mature parents along with a support network of friends and family, ideally including some good men.

7

···

LEGAL AND MORAL ASPECTS OF
BEING A SINGLE MOTHER BY CHOICE

The legal issues surrounding single parenthood are constantly being redefined. When discussing this area of family law it is difficult to generalize since there are many differences among states. There are also new issues being raised every day as families change and modern medical technology makes things possible that were inconceivable (sorry, an irresistible pun!) years ago. Laws that are being enforced today could be changed tomorrow, and there is no way to predict how any particular judge will rule or interpret the laws. So keep in mind that we are on shaky ground when we discuss law. Change is the only thing that is dependable in this area. With that in mind, here are some general guidelines as to what the experiences of SMCs have been thus far with the legal system.

Except for the unknown donor whose sperm is used in donor insemination, in most states an unmarried biological parent who is able and willing to prove paternity has *exactly* the same rights and responsibilities as a married biological parent. There is little or no difference in the eyes of the law. If one parent tries to prevent the other parent from exercising those rights, as is usually the case when an SMC and a known donor draw up an agreement, that is fine only as long as it is not challenged in court. However, if there is a court challenge because one of the parties changes his or her mind, a judge will rarely permit the child's rights to be denied. The law is written to protect children, and according to the law a child has the right to support and visitation from both parents. In many cases, child support payment is a requirement in order for the parent to exercise his paternal rights. Keep in mind that even if you do not want the father to be involved, he can become so if he wants to and if he establishes paternity.

Paternity is usually established by an HLA test, which is considered 100 percent conclusive for establishing nonpaternity and 99 percent conclusive for establishing paternity in most states. Paternity can also be established by a DNA test. Blood tests were formerly not considered very dependable because they merely compared blood types, but today, because of advances in testing technology, they can compare genetic data on a much more precise level and are highly reliable.

What do the laws concerning children and parents mean for you as an SMC? If you conceived with a man and want him to pay child support, you have that legal right, but keep in mind that by requesting or suing him for child support you will also be acknowledging his paternity and thus are opening the door to his exercising all his rights, including visiting and having an ongoing relationship with the child. You will have to weigh your desire or need for child support against the potential advantages or difficulties of the father becoming a participant in your child's life. Particulars such as how involved with one another you and the father were and how near to each other you live are also a factor in how involved he might want to become.

You may welcome his involvement, assuming that he is a

decent and reasonable human being. But if he is abusive or dangerous, you might want to consider whether or not you want him to know that you have borne his child. Do you know him well enough to be sure about how he will react if you tell him? If you definitely do not want the father to be involved and you never tell anyone who he is or tell him about your pregnancy or try to get support from him, there is little chance that he will be a participant in the child's life.

IF THE FATHER KNOWS ABOUT THE CHILD

Many women who become SMCs by conceiving with a man they know erroneously believe that they can go on with their lives free of any involvement with the father. If the father is aware that you have borne his child and wants to become involved, he can go to court, establish paternity by an HLA test, and ask for his parental rights. Some SMCs worry about the father trying to get custody, but that is much more difficult than getting visitation. He would have to make an extremely strong case to prove that he would be a better parent. The fact that he might make more money or have a more luxurious lifestyle would not be sufficient. If he tried to prove that you are an incompetent mother, he would have to demonstrate that you are doing something illegal or immoral or which interferes with your being a good parent to your child, such as drug addiction, alcoholism, or prostitution. Despite fears to the contrary and the recent growing trend for fathers to seek custody of even quite young children, most judges still believe that a young child belongs with his mother and are not eager to remove a young child from a mother's custody without very strong reasons.

Even if the father is uninterested in custody or visitation, he still has the legal responsibility of paying child support if you demand it. However, if you deliberately chose to become a single mother without allowing the father to participate in that decision, most people feel it is immoral to then turn around and sue the father for child support. Nevertheless, it is legally possible to do so. Keep in mind that you usually cannot have the support payments without also being willing to allow visitation, so even if the father is uninterested now, if you sue for child support you are opening the door for his future involvement in your life and your child's life should he ever change his mind. Of course if he is a good person, this could be a real plus for your child.

A Prenatal Contract Is Not a Legal Document

A contract or agreement between you and the biological father may or may not stand up if challenged in court if it denies any of the father's or the child's rights. It is still a very good idea to draw up such an agreement so that both you and the biological father have a clear understanding of one another's intentions and so you each have an outline of what you expect of one another. But that is what it is—an agreement between the two of you. It probably will not be binding, even if drawn up by an attorney. Two sample agreements can be found in Appendix C of this book.

IF THE FATHER DOES NOT KNOW ABOUT THE CHILD

If the father does not know that you conceived and bore his child, and you do not want him to know, he still has the same legal rights as any father if he should find out about the situation and establish paternity at a future time. If you are worried about his involvement, be sure you don't unwittingly open the door and make it easy for him to establish paternity. Do not put anything in writing referring to his being the father, tell no one about his identity, do not give the child his last name, and do not put his name on the birth certificate even if that is possible in your state—just leave that spot blank on the form.

Why would someone not want to tell a man that she has borne his child? You may have decided not to tell him because you felt he would not be a good influence on the child, or that his behavior might disrupt your and your child's lives. Or you may fear that he will sue for custody or demand joint custody. Remember that the right to have both parents involved is the *child's* right and that the court is concerned with what is in the *child's* best interest. You cannot deny a child access to one of his parents without a very good reason, and the court would have to agree with your reasons if it were to support your wishes to prevent the father from participating in his child's life. The father also has rights if he has established paternity, and the court will not deny him his rights without good reason.

Most SMCs are employed and support themselves and their child, but there is always a possibility of your needing help if you run into unexpected financial difficulties. If you lose your job and have to ask for financial assistance from a public agency (public assistance) you will be expected to provide the name of the child's father, and the public welfare agency will usually try to find him and require him to pay child support (if he is financially able to do so) before they give you any assistance. They will tell the father of the child's existence regardless of whatever wishes you may have had to keep that information from him.

Does a woman have the moral right to raise her child without the father ever knowing of his existence? There are some circumstances where that can be argued. Some women would prefer raising their child alone to involving a man with whom they may have had a brief affair but whom they do not want as a father for their child. A woman might feel this way particularly if the pregnancy was accidental and she conceived with someone who she never dreamed would be in her life for more than a short time, much less be the father of her child. (This is one of the main reasons why many women prefer to conceive by donor insemination with an unknown donor— there is no cause to be concerned about the father unexpectedly reappearing in your life.) Another way to prevent such problems is to avoid having sex with anyone whom you would not be willing to have as an active participant in your child's life, although this is not very practical advice—we do not usually choose our social partners on the basis of their potential as fathers!

However, regardless of your wishes, remember that if the father learns of the fact that you bore his child he can claim his rights. What he would have to do is legally establish that he is the father, usually by a blood test, and then you and he (or your attorneys) would have to work out some sort of mutually agreeable visiting arrangement. Keep in mind that if the father establishes paternity, you then have the right to child support.

If you and the father lost touch before you realized you were pregnant, there may not be much you can do about it, but when your child asks you, let's say at age fifteen, whether his father knew about his existence, and you deliberately did not tell his father, how will you feel about answering that question? How do you think the father would feel if he learned that you had given birth to his child? Some men would very much want to know and would feel that by not telling them you had robbed them of the opportunity and experience of being a parent. Other men would feel resentful and angry that you had used them without their knowledge or consent to fulfill your own desires to have a child. Your child may wish that you had told his father, thinking that if he had known he would have been eager to be a participant in the child's life.

Some SMCs tell the father simply to avoid the possibility of the child's being angry at them later on for not having told him. By letting the father know, they leave him with the decision of whether or not to get involved. Others do not tell the father if they believe he would be a disruptive factor in their lives and hope that the child will understand when he or she is older.

It is hard to imagine that any child would prefer that his mother not tell his father that he exists. I tend to agree with what my son said at age twelve, when I asked him whether he thought a child would prefer that his mother tell his father of his existence or not. He said, "She should tell him because then he can choose whether or not he wants to get back together with her or be part of the child's life or say, 'Forget it.'" Unless there are serious extenuating circumstances, as mentioned earlier, I think it is only fair for a father to have the opportunity to decide whether or not he wants to parent, and it is also important for the child's sake that his father have been given the option to be in his life. If you feel strongly that you want to parent alone, without any potential complications with the father, your best method of conception is via a sperm bank.

INHERITANCE RIGHTS

A child can usually inherit from her father once paternity has been established, regardless of whether or not her parents were married, even if there was no will—and if the father had a will that refers to a "child" or "children," your child is included whether or not she is referred to by name. However, there are laws in many states that make it impossible for a child born out of wedlock to inherit from a grandparent unless the grandparent specifies that child *by name* in his or her will. If the child is named in the will, there is no inheritance problem. Your child is *your* legal heir, but if he was born out of wedlock he may not be the legal heir of your parents.

Accordingly, if you are not certain how your parents' wills are written, it is important that you look into it and make sure that your parents are not unwittingly depriving your child of an inheritance they want her to have.

Also keep in mind that if you have a will, you have to designate your child as your heir in order for her to inherit from you.

LEGAL ASPECTS OF ADOPTION

U.S. adoption laws and regulations vary greatly from state to state and are constantly in flux, so it is *essential* to get advice about the current situation from a local adoption support group in your area and/or an attorney who has adoption experience in your state. (See Appendix B for a list of adoption support groups and resources.)

If you are interested in an international adoption, since the laws vary from country to country and also from year to year within any one country, it is important to be in touch with adoption support groups so that you are sure you have the most current information. As described earlier in the case of Harriet, the adopting SMC, it is not unheard of to have a country permit adoptions by singles for a while and then change its policy to allow only married couples to adopt from the country. The country may even revert to a more liberal policy at a later date. Sometimes the changes in policy have to do with the country's local politics and sometimes the reasons are unclear, especially to an outsider, and there is often no way to predict how or when or what the next change will be.

There are also differences from state to state as to the specific time period in which a birth mother can change her mind before the adoption is finalized. In Texas there is no waiting period, for example, while in California the waiting period is two years. Remember that in some states independent adoption is not legal. It is essential to check with a lawyer in your state for the most current information.

In recent years courts in some states have ruled in favor of permitting gay and lesbian couples to adopt and it appears that the courts have taken seriously the research that indicates that children who were raised by homosexual couples do as well in their development as those who were raised by heterosexual couples, and that these children are no more likely to become homosexual than are any other children.

Similarly, courts in some states, such as Vermont, New York, and New Jersey, have ruled that if a gay woman gives birth to a child, her lover can adopt the child so that they can share custody as would any heterosexual married couple. This is important because in the event that the child's biological mother should die, the adoptive mother automatically would have custody of and responsibility for the child. In the past, this was problematic, as sometimes the child's biological grandparents or another relative would sue for custody. Even when the mother had specified in her will that her lover should be the legal guardian, there was no way of knowing whether or not the relatives would challenge that and if it would be supported by the court. If the lover is also the legal adoptive parent of the child, there is considerably less chance of someone else obtaining custody. As with so many other aspects of adoption, the laws relating to gay and lesbian parental rights are constantly changing and you need to stay in touch with adoption support groups and your lawyer in order to assure that you have the most current information.

Finally, remember that as a single parent it is essential that you have a will and name a guardian for your child. Do this before the child is born or as soon as you adopt, and update it as your circumstances change. Make sure the guardian you choose is willing to accept the responsibility. Try to keep your financial affairs in order. It may be difficult to think about these matters, but in the unlikely event of your premature death, the arrangements you have made will protect your child.

8

. . . .

SOCIAL LIFE AND
THE SINGLE MOTHER BY CHOICE

We all know that we need to have a good balance between work and play in order to have a healthy life. We also need to work out how to have a balanced social life as an SMC—we need some time with other adults with children and some time with other adults without children.

SOCIAL LIFE WITH OTHER PARENTS AND CHILDREN

Particularly in the early years of motherhood, you may find that you begin to crave the company of other adults after you have spent a couple of hours alone with your child. This is perfectly normal, not just for SMCs but for all mothers. Being with a baby is very intense and demands that you use parts of yourself that you are not accustomed to using as an adult— nonverbal, almost primitive levels of relating and com- municating. You also have to be constantly aware of where your baby or toddler is, what he is doing, and what he needs or will be needing, all of which is very draining. Being with another adult or another parent who also has a child dilutes the intensity of your mother-child dyad and simultaneously enables you to enjoy the social and intellectual stimulation of adult company. By so doing, you can refuel and get reenergized as you continue to care for your child.

If you have a baby or toddler you will find that you most need to have other adults around during weekends and vacations because of the long stretches of time that have to be filled. One person alone with such a young child can burn out all too quickly. New mothers often find it easy to make "mother friendships" at this time in their lives because they feel such a strong need for the company of other adults, particularly other mothers. Many SMCs tell me that they were surprised that they were able to enjoy the company of women with whom they had little else in common besides being a mother simply because that bond was so important at that particular time. If you have similar parenting styles or your children are comfortable with one another, that can be enough of a basis for a mother friendship. If you have other things in common as well, it may develop into a more lasting friendship, but often these friendships die out once the children are older, especially if the children go to different schools and start making their own friends, separate from your circle.

It may be easier to find other SMCs who want to socialize with you than it is to find married parents. Married couples have one another's company and accordingly they may not feel as strong a need to have another adult around as does an SMC who is alone. Married people also tend to socialize more with other couples, as some couples tend to feel a little awkward with a single woman. Perhaps the man in the couple may prefer to socialize with another couple so that he can have another man to relate to, and a married mother may feel a little threatened by having a single woman around her husband. However, having some "couple friends" does provide a chance for your child to see what dads are like and for you to have two other adults to chat with while the children play. (Sometimes I say, only half in jest, that every child should have three parents so that two can chat while one is watching the children.)

If you have been able to find or create a network of other single mothers with young children, you will probably have many opportunities to get together and do things that are fun and relaxing for you and your child. In the first year or so, just being able to hang out with other mothers who have a child around the same age can be at least a restful time and at best a wonderful opportunity to get to know some new, interesting people. Your child will have the advantage of becoming familiar with and comfortable at a number of other people's homes and in addition, this circle of friends can become a built-in network to provide your child with playmates, baby-sitters, and friends for sleepovers as he or she gets older.

As your child enters school, she will start making her own friends, separate from you. You will find yourself calling parents who are virtual strangers to you and introducing yourself as "Julie's mother." There may be some awkward times at this stage because many of the parents to whom you introduce yourself will have no inkling that you are an SMC and they will often assume that you are married (or that you were married and are now divorced or widowed). You might want to explain your situation to these parents in front of your child so you can provide her with a model of how to handle those kinds of questions. Afterward you can discuss any questions she may have about what you said. However, keep in mind that you never know how people will react, and if you have the very first discussion of the subject when your child is around, be prepared in case the other family's response is not a positive one.

There is a definite case to be made for giving your child the opportunity to hear you explain your kind of family to others, especially if you are able to do it in a fairly comfortable way and the people you are telling are not excessively emotional in their response. It probably takes a little bit of social intuition to be able to sense how the other parents are going to respond, but in my experience this is usually something at which SMCs become fairly adept. It is possible that you will guess incorrectly at times, but as long as you are there to be a buffer for your child, and *you* can handle the unpleasant response, it will not have a lasting negative impact on your child. It is always a good idea to follow up on any discussion about your family that your child overhears with a chat together about how he interpreted or understood what he heard.

SOCIAL LIFE WITH OTHER ADULTS

There are times when you need to forget that you are a mother and be just with other adults, to have friends (either men or women) who are not in any way connected with you as a mother but who perhaps share other interests with you such as a career or hobby. We also need to make sure that we give ourselves time to look for and enjoy the company of men, as it is sometimes all too easy to get immersed in motherhood and forget that we also are sexual beings.

Most SMCs find that it is relatively easy to keep their professional or career contacts going, partly because most of us go back to work fairly soon after the baby arrives, and also because we need to maintain those relationships as part of our work lives, which sooner or later we will be resuming. Since you know you will eventually be returning to work, you realize that you *have* to keep this part of your life going, whereas when it comes to hobbies and strictly personal friends, it is easier to let them slide when time and energy are tight.

It may be that you will naturally return to your hobbies and personal interests, although perhaps with less frequency as you have less time available. Some mothers find that now that they have so little free time, they are no longer interested in some of the things they used to do or some of the friends they used to see. Before becoming a mother you may have had to work hard to fill up all your free time, but now that you are a mother you will only have time for a few of the many things that were important to you before the baby arrived. Prioritizing is the key to not feeling totally frazzled and to making the best use of your limited available time and energy. Most of the SMCs with whom I have discussed this say that it is amazing to realize how much their priorities changed after becoming a mother, and how much richer their lives felt with a baby at the center of everything. This is often particularly the case with regard to dating.

DATING AND THE SINGLE MOTHER BY CHOICE

Many SMCs report that they find dating to be much more enjoyable after becoming mothers than it was before. The reason is very simply that the pressure is off. Having already had a baby, they now can relax about that and take their time having fun and getting to know the man they are dating. Men I see in my psychotherapy practice have commented on how rough it can be dating women in their thirties because the women are getting frantic about their biological clocks running down, and, not surprisingly, this pressure is conveyed to the men.

However, dating as an SMC is complicated and becomes increasingly so as your child gets older, because your child's needs become more of a factor as he becomes more of a person. If you start to have a serious relationship, you will have to face questions of priorities (your child's needs versus your boyfriend's needs) that you did not have to worry about when you and your child were a twosome. Many of the issues are the same for an SMC as for other kinds of single mothers but there is one major difference—an SMC's child does not usually already have a dad in the picture, whereas the children of other single mothers usually do.

From a man's point of view, if he is interested in being a primary figure in the child's life, the fact that your child does not have a dad can be a plus because there is room for him to step into the role. On the other hand, if your child is yearning for a dad you may find her pressuring you to provide her with one, and sometimes kids can be embarrassingly direct. One SMC in Boston told me that her five-year-old daughter went right up to a nice-looking man who was in the park with his toddler and asked him, "Would you like to be my dad? My mom hasn't been able to find one for me."

DATING WHEN YOU HAVE A BABY

Some SMCs only half-jokingly say that in the first year of motherhood, their idea of a perfect date is to go right to bed—alone. All they want is a good night's sleep. But some new moms are lucky enough to be getting a decent amount of sleep and do start dating fairly soon. If you are one of these, there are a few factors that make dating at this time different from before you were a mother.

The biggest issue is that the baby at this stage is unpredictable. If you are lucky the baby will be oblivious to your date when he comes to pick you up and will be sleeping when you return. If not, your date will have to be patient enough to wait for you while you get the baby to sleep. On the other hand, you may be all ready to go out, the doorbell may even be ringing, and you will suddenly realize that your baby has a raging fever. Or you may come home in a romantic mood with your date and find that the baby has enjoyed a wonderful nap while you were gone and is now all ready for playtime and wants you to join him! It will take a fairly mature man to be able to deal with these kinds of complications, but then you wouldn't want an immature man in your life anyway, would you?

Another small but embarrassing problem that may occur if you are breast-feeding is that your breast milk may suddenly start to flow during a romantic moment or if you start thinking about your baby, and you will experience a wet stain growing on the front of your dress. It takes a certain kind of flair to "act casual" as you are getting wetter and the stain is getting bigger!

DATING WHEN YOU HAVE A TODDLER

During the toddler years your child will probably be very interested in the man you are dating and may try to compete with you for his attention, demanding that he play with her rather than you. Whether she says so or not, she will probably assume that the kind of person she has often seen at friends' houses has finally turned up at your house, too—in other words, she will assume in some sense that this man is her dad. You can try to correct or prevent this belief until you are blue in the face, but there is no way you can make your child give up her fantasies.

The typical toddler's unquestioning willingness to attach to any man can be problematic if you allow your date to meet or spend time with your child, because your child may attach to him before you have been able to get to know him and decide whether or not you want him in your life. It is sometimes easier, for this reason, to meet your dates outside of your home for as long as it may take for you to have a good idea of where the relationship may be going. You can explain to your dates, if asked, that you want to keep your child from getting involved in your social life.

You will need to protect your child from getting attached to a series of men who then disappear from his life. Some SMCs feel comfortable bringing their beaus into the home after the first few dates but others keep them out of the home and away from their children until they are clear that they have found someone with whom they are going to have a relationship of at least a fairly long-lasting nature. You may feel this kind of behavior is overly cautious or unfair to your dates, and of course at some point you will want them to meet your child and see how they interact with each other, but there are some sound reasons for waiting, the primary one being to protect your young child from going through painful and unnecessary losses.

Why Keep Your Dates Away from Your Child?
Young children (toddlers, preschool, and early school years) get very attached to people quite readily and if you don't protect your child from getting attached to your dates he will suffer some degree of rejection and abandonment when you and the man stop seeing each other. A child has no ability to conceptualize or understand relationships in the early years, and his experience will be that the person has suddenly disappeared. He may even feel that somehow it was his fault. To make it even more complicated, the child will be confused and upset about why the person left, but as a toddler or very young child he doesn't yet have the capacity to talk about hurt feelings the way an adult can.

If Your Child Dislikes Your Date/Boyfriend
Another possible scenario that can unfold, especially with children of school age, is that your child does not like the man whom you are dating or feels threatened that the man is taking your attention away from him. He may cry when the man arrives to take you out and if you try to include him in your relationship by planning family outings, he may be obnoxious and do his best to ruin the day. He may go so far as to tell you that he hates the man and beg you not to see him. This kind of reaction has to be taken seriously and evaluated. Is the man, in fact, not nice to your child or frightening to him in some way? Or is your child just wanting his time with you to be exclusive and having trouble sharing you with someone else? Keep in mind that our SMC children are usually used to having us all to themselves. Does he react that way with

female friends or other men who want your attention, or is it just with this particular man?

Obviously, if a man is not nice to your child, you should not try to include him in your family. On the other hand, if he is genuinely nice and you really care about him, and you feel that your child is simply having a hard time adjusting to sharing you, you will need to help him with the adjustment. You might arrange to chat with your son or daughter at a relaxed, cozy time when the man is not around. Reassure your child that you will always love him, no matter whether you also love a man or not. Explain that this man makes you feel happy (assuming that he does, or else you would not be having this discussion) and that it is important that you be happy because it helps you to be a good mother. He will likely protest that he tries to make you happy, and why isn't that enough? You will need to assure him that indeed he does make you very happy, but that adults also need other adults to make them happy. Make sure that you and your child have time alone together in addition to the time you spend as a threesome, particularly during the early phases of your new relationship, and try to be especially attentive during those times.

Relationship Blues

If you are having problems with a man, try not to involve your child in the ups and downs of the relationship. Children cannot really understand such things and will be likely to simply get angry at the man for upsetting you. This can cause problems if you and he work out your problems and ultimately get together, as your child may feel she has to protect you from this potentially hurtful man.

You will probably not be able to hide your distress from your child when things aren't going well or if the relationship ends, but you do not have to go into detail about what is bothering you either. It is not appropriate to use your child as a confidante. You can let your child know that you are sad, and reassure her that it has nothing to do with her. When you are calmer, however long that may take, then you can explain to her that you and the man have decided not to continue seeing each other, if that is the way it worked out. If she also had an emotional involvement with him, you need to evaluate how it should be handled between them.

Your Child's Relationship with Your Ex-boyfriend

We all know how much the end of an affair can hurt, even for an adult, so imagine how a child is likely to feel. If it was a lengthy and caring quasi-parental relationship, you might discuss with the man how he feels about continuing it with the child even though you and he are not going to be involved any longer. Sometimes the relationship with the child has become important enough to the man to warrant his trying to maintain it to some degree, as in a divorce situation. However, it is also possible that he will be unable or unwilling to do so, and in that case you will have to help your child grieve over the loss while you are also going through your own grieving.

If it was not such an involved relationship, then you will just need to help your child learn that not all relationships are forever. Often he will blame himself, as children tend to do, for the relationship ending and carry around an unspoken burden of guilt. If this guilt is not addressed it may manifest itself later on in depression, self-defeating behaviors, or difficulty in sustaining lasting relationships. It is important to talk it through with your child and reassure him that the relationship's ending was not because of anything he said or did. You may be surprised at how many times you will need to go over and over the situation with your child as he grapples to understand what happened to this person.

Sex and the SMC

When you are seeing someone with whom you want to have a sexual involvement, you will have to face the question of where and when you can have sex if you have a small child in your home. There is no absolute agreement among experts as to what effect it has on a child to know that a man is sharing his mother's bed. Some feel that it is not a problem if the man has become a part of the family first and if there is a committed relationship. Others feel that if you do not want your child to have premarital sex, you should not let your child see *you* having sex outside of marriage, because you need to set an example. However, just about everyone agrees that a child should not be allowed to witness a parent having sex and that it is not healthy for your child to see a series of men in your bed.

Ideally, if you develop a serious involvement with someone, you will find a way to have privacy to explore the sexual part of your relationship, perhaps in his home or while your child is at someone else's home for a visit. After the age of three or four your child will start liking to have overnights with a willing friend or relative. If your child's friend also has a single mom, you can work out a system of swapping overnights. When and if the time comes that you decide to bring the man into your bedroom, be sure that you have first brought him into your home and given your child enough time to become comfortable with him as someone who is a part of your family.

One last suggestion—put a lock on your bedroom door. If you do not, you can be sure that at some point your child will walk in on you while you and the man are in some state of undress or in the middle of having sex. If your child is old enough to question the reason for the lock, explain that adults sometimes need privacy. An SMC to whom I spoke about this told me that her precocious daughter, age eight, responded by saying, "Oh, so you and Jim can have sex, right?" What can you say to such directness except "Yes"?

While having a social life has its complications, it is essential to your having a reasonably well-balanced life and is also important for your child to learn to be a social being in the world. Many SMCs find that they make a whole new set of friends because of becoming mothers, and that, rather than having less of a social life than before, they have a fuller and larger one. And don't forget that as your child gets older, she will also have her own social life, separate from yours, so you should be careful not to let yourself become overly dependent upon her company. That way, when she starts to spend less time with you, you will have a life of your own already in place and the separation will be less painful.

IF YOU MARRY

It is possible that at some point you may decide to get married, and that decision will bring with it both emotional and legal issues. Ideally, if you have been dating someone seriously, you and your child have already begun to make some adjustments in your relationship because of your involvement with your lover. Children are usually sticklers for routines and get anxious when their routines change. If you talk about changes that are forthcoming about a week or two ahead of time for a preschool child and a few months before for an older child, that will help them prepare for the changes. You may be moving to a new house or a new town and there may be a new day-care arrangement. These changes, and even a wedding in which the child will take part, while a happy occasion, can be somewhat stressful for a child. Generally speaking, the younger the child, the more difficult a time he will have with changes.

EMOTIONAL ISSUES

The most important change that comes about when an SMC becomes seriously involved with someone and marries him is that the child is now part of a threesome, whereas before the mother and child were basically a twosome. More than most children, the children of SMCs are used to being the main focus of their mother's attention at home, and they rarely have to compete for it—their mother is there for them and for no one else a good deal of the time. Once a man becomes a part of the family, that balance changes and the child now has a rival for her mother's attention. This has its positives, especially for a child around four or five, who is close to being developmentally ready to share. The child will surely benefit from her mother's happiness, and from having another adult who loves her in her life. She will have to learn to compete for and share her mother's attention and to occasionally put her needs on hold while Mom is attending to her husband's needs. The mother will have to insist on some private time and perhaps put a lock on the bedroom door. While this may be a blow to a child who has been used to always having access to her mother and to her room, it is also important for her to learn about people's need for privacy and to discover that at times she can rely on herself to solve a problem.

The change is much harder for a child under four whose

world has always been child-centered and who may not yet be verbal enough to really talk about his feelings when the situation changes at home. Because he is less verbal, a younger child may have tantrums or regress to a younger level of functioning in such ways as bed-wetting, asking for a bottle when he has been using a cup, and thumb-sucking or other behaviors that he had outgrown. These are the only ways he may have available to comfort himself, and they should not be treated as disciplinary problems. You will need to spend a good deal of time reassuring your child that you still love him, that you understand that this is a big change, and that you are still his mother even though the family has grown larger. (See also the discussion on page 198, "If Your Child Dislikes Your Date/Boyfriend.")

The fact that there may be a somewhat stressful period of adjustment should not be a major problem—this, too, will pass if you continue to provide your child with a sense of security and love. And the fact that you and your family have the commitment of another loving person will more than balance whatever growing pains your child may experience.

LEGAL ISSUES

If you marry, your new husband may want to legally adopt your child. This is an important step and one whose symbolism can bring a family closer together. If your child was conceived by donor insemination there should be no obstacles in the way of your husband adopting, because the donor surrendered his parental rights at the time he agreed to be a donor. However, if the father was someone you knew, the situation is more complicated.

As with other legal issues, you should check with a lawyer

who is familiar with family law in your state, because the laws vary from state to state. In some states it may be possible for your husband to adopt your child if the child's father can be said to have abandoned the child or if the father is willing to sign a form consenting to the adoption. However, if he chooses to fight the adoption and refuses to give up his parental rights, you will have to go to court, where a decision will be made based on the particulars of your case.

If your new husband legally adopts your child, he or she becomes your husband's child in every legal sense, including rights to inherit and to receive social security or veterans' benefits.

If adoption turns out not to be possible because of the father's refusal to cooperate, your husband can still designate your child in his will *by name* to receive a portion of his estate. He can also make the child a beneficiary of a trust fund and of his insurance policies if he wishes. And the fact that your husband cannot legally adopt your child, if that is the case, does not in any way prevent the two of them from developing strong emotional ties, assuming that they have developed a good relationship.

IF YOU DO NOT MARRY

You may have always assumed that at some point in your life you would marry. Having a baby on your own might have seemed like a temporary diversion on the path to marriage, simply putting the cart before the horse, so to speak. However, as your child grows up you may find that you are less interested in marriage than you were earlier.

Most SMCs discover that they feel more relaxed about

dating and less pressured to figure out whether each man they meet is "Mr. Right" since they have already started their families. Not *needing* to marry allows you to take your time and look at a man more objectively in order to decide whether or not you *want* to marry him, whether or not he is a person whom you feel you can have a loving relationship with. You simply may feel more freedom to be really selective about whom you might consider marrying. And with that freedom to choose out of want rather than need, you may find that "Mr. Right" is difficult (sometimes impossible) to find, and that meanwhile you are content to go on with your life as a single parent. As one SMC said to me, "When I was single—I mean before I had my daughter—I felt much less comfortable being alone. Now I feel I'm okay either with a man or without one. It is not a major issue in my life anymore." Her slip of the tongue reflects what many SMCs feel: they don't feel single, at least not in the way that they used to, once they have a child. They are, and feel like, a family. Yet we are still single, and as our children grow up we have to depend more and more upon ourselves and our friends for our socializing needs. Make sure that you are not being a pseudo-couple with your child, since that would not be good for either one of you, and remember that your child's increasing independence is a gift to you. You can begin to pick up old interests or develop new ones that you may have wanted to include in your life but had no time for when your child was younger.

Coming to terms with staying single involves another adjustment as once again we are not fitting that profile of what was expected of us or what we expected of ourselves at an earlier time in our lives. We are not following the traditional path. Our culture is very "coupled" and people who are content to not be married are sometimes looked at as curiosities. Often there are questions—"Is he (or she) gay?" being a typical one—and assumptions—"You must feel so sad that you've never married." Discussing these concerns with close friends and family can give them a better understanding of what you really feel about being single.

Often you will need to go through a period of grieving over this disappointment, if it is a disappointment to you, just as you had to grieve over not having had a child within a traditional marriage. Interestingly, some SMCs have told me that being in touch with and focusing on their grief about not having married has helped them to empathize with their childrens' feelings about not having had a dad. Both are experiences that have the potential to bring a great deal of pleasure into one's life, and both are experiences that we and/or our children have missed out on. Once the grieving is faced and done, we can be free to more fully enjoy those other wonderful aspects of life that we do have—our children, our careers, our friends and family, or whatever else we may enjoy.

Being single today is not necessarily a lonely existence, nor is it perceived as a sign of failure, as used to be the case. (When did you last hear someone use the term "old maid"?) More and more women are saying that being single is a state that they are able to appreciate and enjoy, and they surely feel it is better than marrying for the sake of marrying (or because of societal or family pressure to conform) when there is not real love.

So if you have decided not to marry, or if it looks as though you may not find the right man to share your life with on a permanent basis, enjoy yourself. Enjoy your own company and that of your child and other loved ones, enjoy dating and socializing, and know that you are one of an increasing number of women who would rather stay single than marry someone whom she does not love.

SINGLE MOTHERHOOD CAN BE
A WONDERFUL CHOICE

People often ask me if I have any regrets about having chosen to become a single mother, and I do not. I felt strongly that this course was the right one for me, and I still do. However, when I made the decision to go ahead with my pregnancy nearly seventeen years ago I really had no idea of what lay in store for me. I naïvely thought that parenthood would be easy, and instead I found it to be the hardest thing I have ever done—a humbling experience. Thankfully, it has also been the most rewarding. It gave me a unique opportunity to get to know myself—both my abilities and my limitations—and become a more mature person. I was able to develop more patience and more realistic expectations of myself and others. I deepened my understanding of people, particularly parents and children, and gained greater respect for the differences among us.

But most of all, being a parent changed my perspective on life, as I realized that loving those close to me, my son first and foremost among them, was what brought me the most satisfaction. Thanks to him, I was able to feel content with myself and my life in a way that I never was able to before.

I guess I should admit that I was not totally honest when I said I had no regrets—the one regret I have is that I was not able to have a second child to be able to enjoy without all the inevitable worries of a first-time mother. But that is a small regret, and I do thoroughly enjoy the dog we got when I realized I wasn't going to have another child—and also the cat we got when the urge for another baby resurfaced again a few years ago.

My last word on the subject—follow your own path. If it is single motherhood, enjoy it. If it is not, see what other adventures might be out there waiting for you, and live them.

SPERM BANKS AND FERTILITY RESOURCES

IMPORTANT: These are in zip code order, with Canadian and UK resources at the end. Policies change all the time, so contact them to ask for more information about their programs or whether they have ID release or "yes" donors, photos of donors, etc. This information is current as of 2007.

California Cryobank
950 Massachusetts Avenue
Cambridge, MA 02139
(617) 497-8646
www.cryobank.com

New England Cryogenics
153 Needham Street, Building #1
Newton, MA 02464
(617) 262-3311, (800) 991-4999

Coastal Women's Health Care
96 Campus Drive, U.S. Route One
Scarborough, ME 04074
(207) 885-8400
www.coastalwhc.com

U. of Conn. Health Center
263 Farmington Avenue
Farmington, CT 06030
(860) 679-2000
www.uchc.edu

Biogenetics
1130 Route 22 West
P.O. Box 1290
Mountainside, NJ 07092
(800) 637-7776
www.sperm1.com/biogenetics

Repro Lab
336 East 30th Street
New York, NY 10016
(212) 779-3988
www.reprolabinc.com

Pittsburgh Cryobank
4415 Fifth Avenue, Suite 161
Pittsburgh, PA 15213
(412) 687-0335
www.pittsburghcryobank.com

Mainline Reproductive Science Center
950 West Valley Road
Wayne, PA 19087
(610) 964-9663

Hospital of the U. of Penn.
3400 Spruce Street
Philadelphia, PA 19104
(215) 662-6100
www.pennhealth.com/hup

Women's Institute
815 Locust Street
Philadelphia, PA 19107
(215) 922-2206
www.womensinstitute.org

Washington Fertility Study Center
2600 Virginia Ave. N.W., Suite 500
Washington, DC 20037
(202) 333-3100

Columbia Hospital for Women
Division of RE and Infertility
2440 M Street N.W.
Washington, DC 20037
(202) 293-6567

Genetics and in Vitro
Fertilization Institute
3020 Javier Road
Fairfax, VA 22031
(800) 552-4363
www.givf.com

Fairfax Cryobank
3015 Williams Drive, Suite 110
Fairfax, VA 22031
(800) 338-8407
www.fairfaxcryobank.com

North Carolina Center for
Reproductive Medicine
400 Asheville Ave., Suite 200
Cary, NC 27511
(919) 233-1680, (800) 933-7202
www.nccrm.com

Southeastern Fertility Center
1375 Hospital Drive
Mount Pleasant, SC 29464
(843) 881-3900
www.sefertility.com

Feminist Women's Health
1924 Cliff Valley Way
Atlanta, GA 30329
(404) 248-5445
www.feministcenter.org

Xytex Corporation
1776 Peachtree Street N.E.
Suite L6
Atlanta, GA 30309
(404) 881-0426
www.xytex.com

Xytex Corporation
1100 Emmett Street
Augusta, GA 30904
(800) 277-3210, (706) 733-0130

Florida Institute for
Reproductive Medicine
836 Prudential Drive, Suite 902
Jacksonville, FL 32207
(904) 399-5620
www.firmjax.com

U. of Alabama at Birmingham:
Dept. of Reproductive
Endocrinology and Infertility
1610 Center Street, Suite 201
Mobile, AL 36604
(251) 415-1496
www.southalabama.edu/
usahealthsystem/womenshealth

Cryobiology
4830-D Knightsbridge
Columbus, OH 43214
(800) 359-4375
www.cryobio.com

International Cryogenics
189 Townsend, Suite 203
Birmingham, MI 48009
(248) 644-5822
www.internationalcryo.com

U. of Michigan Hospitals
1500 East Medical Center Drive
Ann Arbor, MI 48109
(734) 936-4000
www.med.umich.edu

Cryogenic Laboratories
1944 Lexington Avenue
North Roseville, MN 55113
(612) 489-8000, (800) 466-2796
www.cryolab.com

Midwest Fertility Center
4333 Main Street
Downers Grove, IL 60515
(800) 244-0212
www.midwestfertilitycenter.com

Illinois Masonic Med. Center
836 West Wellington
Chicago, IL 60657
(773) 975-1600
www.advocatehealth.com/immc

Center for Human Reproduction
2825 N. Halsted Street
Chicago, IL 60657
(773) 472-4949
www.centerforhumanreproduction.com

Reproductive Resources
3901 Houma Blvd., Suite 223
Metairie, LA 70006
(504) 454-7973, (800) 227-4561
www.reproductiveresources.com

Fertility Institute of New Orleans
6020 Bullard Avenue
New Orleans, LA 70128
(800) 433-9009
www.fertilityinstitute.com

CryoGam Colorado
2216 Hoffman Drive, Unit B
Loveland, CO 80538
(800) 473-9601
www.cryogam.com

California Cryobank
11915 LaGrange Avenue
Los Angeles, CA 90025
(800) 977-3761
www.cryobank.com

Zygen Labs
16917 Enadia Way
Van Nuys, CA 91406
(800) 255-7242, (818) 705-3600
www.zygen.com

Fertility Center of California
845 West LaVeta Ave., Suite 104
Orange, CA 92868
(714) 744-2040
www.fertilityctr.com

Pacific Reproductive Services
444 Deharo Street, Suite 222
San Francisco, CA 94114
(415) 487-2288
www.hellobaby.com

Sperm Bank of California
2115 Milvia Street
Berkeley, CA 94704
(510) 841-1858
www.thespermbankofca.org

Infertility Network
160 Pickering Street
Toronto, Ontario
(416) 691-3611
www.infertilitynetwork.org

IVF Canada
2347 Kennedy Road, Suite 304
Scarborough, Ontario
(416) 754-8742
www.ivfcanada.com

ReproMed Ltd.
56 Aberfoyle Crescent
Etobicoke, Ontario
(416) 233-8111
www.repromedltd.com

London Health Science Centre
800 Commissioners Road East
London, Ontario
(519) 685-8500
www.lhsc.on.ca

Genesis Fertility Centre
555 W. 12th Avenue, Rm. 550
Vancouver, British Columbia
(604) 879-3032
www.genesis-fertility.com

Donor Conception Network
P.O. Box 7471
Nottingham, NG36ZP
United Kingdom
www.dcnetwork.org

Web site to help readers choose a
sperm bank, and other helpful
information and resources:
www.fertilityplus.org

Online Donor Sibling Registry:
www.groups.yahoo.com/group/
DonorSiblingRegistry/

Online Donor Sibling Registry:
www.donorsiblingregistry.com

SINGLE-PARENT
ADOPTION RESOURCES

National Council for Single Adoptive Parents
P.O. Box 15084
Chevy Chase, MD 20825
www.ncsap.org
Membership provides nationwide information on agencies
that accept single applicants, names of state and local single-
adoptive-parent groups, recommended books, names of prospective or actual adoptive single parents in your state. Also
publishes *Handbook for Single Adoptive Parents.* A great help if
you're at the begining of the adoption process.

Adoptive Families of America, Inc.
2309 Como Ave.
St. Paul, MN 55108
(800) 372-3300
www.adoptivefam.com
National parent support group particularly but not exclu-
sively concerned with special-needs children. Publishes a
newsletter and will send you an outstanding guide to adoption
on request (free, but as good as many costly books).

Child Welfare Information Gateway
U.S. Department of Health and Human Services
1250 Maryland Ave. SW, 8th floor
Washington, DC 20024
(703) 385-7565
(800) 394-3366
www.childwelfare.gov
Has a computerized information data base that contains titles and abstracts of hundreds of adoption documents. You may request searches on many adoption topics and receive computer printouts of the abstracts of relevant articles. You may also request free referrals to adoption agencies, support groups, and experts. An excellent source of information.

International Concerns Committee for Children
911 Cyprus Drive
Boulder, CO 80303
(303) 494-8333
www.iccadopt.org
Provides an annual report with updates on current regulations in various countries regarding foreign adoption.

Latin American Parent's Association
P.O Box 4403
Silver Spring, MD 20904
(301) 431-3407
www.lapa-ncr.org
A national support group that specializes in helping both married and single adoptive parents with Latin American adoptions before, during, and after the actual adoption.

North American Council on Adoptable Children
970 Raymond Ave., Suite 106
St Paul, MN 55114
(651) 644-3036
www.nacac.org
Coalition of adoptive parents' support and advocacy groups. Committed to helping special-needs children waiting for adoption in this country and abroad. They will refer you to resources in your area.

New York Singles Adopting Children
www.groups.yahoo.com/group/SingleAdoptNY
Provides support and information to single adoptive parents in the New York City and Long Island areas. Publishes a bi-monthly newsletter.

Stars of David Inc.
3175 Commercial Ave., Suite 100
Northbrook, IL 60062
(800) STAR 349
www.starsofdavid.org
Information and support for Jewish adoptive families. Local chapters, newsletter.

Families with Children from China (FCC)
P.O. Box 237065
Ansonia Station
New York, NY 10023
www.fccny.com
Has affiliate groups all around the United States and a newsletter.

Chinese Children Adoption International
6920 South Holly Circle
Centennial, CO 80112
(303) 850-9998
www.chinesechildren.org
Loving, competent Chinese couple, with great office staff and network in China.

Families for Russian and Ukrainian Adoption (FRUA)
P.O. Box 2944
Merrifield, VA 22116
(703) 560-6184
www.frua.org
A national group for Eastern European adoptions.

The American Pediatrics Association's adoption Web site:
www.aap.org/sections/adoption

For people just starting to consider adoption:
www.adoptivefamilies.com/adoptionplanner
This is part of Adoptive Family Magazine's annual adoption guide. The planner has a chart comparing different types of adoption (domestic, international, private, etc.) in terms of timeline, cost, age of available children, etc.

. . . .

TWO EXAMPLES OF AN AGREEMENT WITH A KNOWN DONOR

Following are two examples of an agreement that can be drawn up with a known donor. Please keep in mind that NO such agreement can be guaranteed to be legally binding, and most likely will not be.

AGREEMENT ONE: THE FATHER GIVES UP HIS RIGHTS

This AGREEMENT is effective this [   ] day of [   ], 19[ ], by and between Ms. [   ], who will be referred to in this document as RECIPIENT, and Mr. [   ], who will be referred to in this document as DONOR, collectively referred to as the PARTIES.

The PARTIES agree as follows:

1. The PARTIES intend to cooperate in a procedure for artificially inseminating RECIPIENT with DONOR's semen in order to impregnate RECIPIENT and further

intend to arrange their respective rights, obligations and duties with respect to the child(ren) born thereby and with respect to each other. The PARTIES understand and acknowledge that there are many legal relations between each other and as to any child(ren) born as a result of such artificial insemination and that such legal relations are affected by statute, court decisions and by common law, some of which are as yet undecided questions of law and public policy. Nonetheless, both PARTIES desire to enter into this AGREEMENT and to be bound by the terms within it and to act in good faith with respect to such terms and intentions as are expressed in this AGREEMENT. Both PARTIES acknowledge that this AGREEMENT is in the best interests of any child(ren) subsequently born as a result of the contemplated artificial insemination procedure.

2. Each party is currently unmarried and any subsequent marriage does not alter this AGREEMENT nor does any party's subsequent disability or death affect this AGREEMENT.

3. DONOR has and will in good faith provide to RECIPIENT or her designee his semen for use in artificially inseminating RECIPIENT. DONOR will continue to provide his semen two times per month starting around the time of RECIPIENT's ovulation in [month and year], until whichever occurs sooner: RECIPIENT's impregnation or six months from the second donation in [month and year].

4. In exchange for and as consideration for DONOR's semen, RECIPIENT will pay to DONOR a one-time fee of twenty-five dollars ($25).

5. Neither party will request or in any way seek or assist in the establishment or exercise of DONOR's parental rights, duties or obligations. Both parties understand these to include parental inheritance from or to the child(ren); custody; visitation or physical placement with the child(ren); child support; authorization for the child(ren)'s military service, driver's license or marriage; access to medical, dental and educational records; and decisions as to the child(ren)'s health, education, religion or day-to-day activities, protection, training and discipline. It is the intention of the parties that DONOR's parental rights be as if terminated as to any child(ren) born through the contemplated artificial insemination and that all parental rights of RECIPIENT remain fully and completely as to such child(ren).

6. RECIPIENT shall have sole custody and physical placement of any child(ren) born as contemplated in this AGREEMENT and the sole right to exercise parental rights and authority as to said child(ren), unless she specifically states in writing otherwise.

7. DONOR shall not be obligated to pay directly or indirectly for: the pregnancy or birthing expenses, any health or life insurance or any support or expenses whatsoever as to any child(ren) born as a result of the artificial insemination procedure.

8. DONOR's exercise or attempted exercise of any parental rights or parental-like rights as to any child(ren) born as a result of the artificial insemination procedure does not alter this AGREEMENT whether done with or without the consent of RECIPIENT.

9. The PARTIES may disclose this AGREEMENT or its contents or the fact of an actual biological relationship between DONOR and any child(ren) born from this artificial insemination procedure only as follows: as is necessary to effectuate its terms; to each person's own significant other and close friends; and any child(ren) born from the artificial insemination procedure. The PARTIES may not make such disclosures to their parents, other relatives and relative's spouses and children.

10. DONOR may not claim any child(ren) born from the artificial insemination procedure as a dependent for state or federal tax purposes and RECIPIENT may claim any such child(ren).

11. The PARTIES will at all times cooperate in executing any documents necessary to bring about the terms and intent of this AGREEMENT. Upon request by RECIPIENT, DONOR will cooperate in a voluntary legal termination of his parental rights, if any, but RECIPIENT will pay the cost and fees of any such action.

12. This is the complete AGREEMENT of the parties and there are no promises, understandings or representations between the parties other than those expressly stated in this AGREEMENT.

13. The PARTIES are competent adults, under no undue influence, coercion or duress of any kind, and freely and voluntarily enter into this AGREEMENT. Each party understands they have the right and opportunity to consult with an attorney and to the extent they have chosen not to do so, such choice does not enter into it nor does such failure result in construing its terms against the drafting party.

14. Prior to the insemination and as otherwise stated herein, DONOR has provided his blood to a person or agency of RECIPIENT's choice for HIV testing. DONOR will also provide his blood for testing for hepatitis and syphilis. In addition, DONOR will provide his penis culture for testing for gonorrhea. RECIPIENT will pay for all such screening and testing. At all times throughout the insemination period, DONOR will immediately notify RECIPIENT if he has reasonable basis to believe his health and safety, the health and safety of RECIPIENT or the health and safety of the expected child(ren) would be substantially at risk or harmed by his actions or omissions or those of others in relation to his reproductive capacities.

15. Subsequent voiding or unenforceability of a part of these provisions does not render void or unenforceable other provisions herein.

ANOTHER SAMPLE AGREEMENT BETWEEN UNMARRIED PARENTS

This is a much less formal agreement, which some SMCs may prefer.

This is a summary of our discussions that have led to the following mutually agreed upon agreement, which we hope will result in the RECIPIENT's pregnancy, and will be binding on us both forever.

The DONOR agrees to donate sperm without incurring either 1) any financial responsibility whatsoever for any child(ren) conceived with his sperm at any time during that child's minority or thereafter, or 2) any parental rights or responsibilities.

DONOR and RECIPIENT are in agreement on the following:

a)   Only RECIPIENT shall have the right to tell the child the identity of its biological father.

b)   DONOR shall not have any claim to custody of the child and agrees never to make any such claim.

c)   RECIPIENT shall not have or make any claim to financial support from DONOR for the child or herself. Further, in the event of RECIPIENT's death, no member of her family nor any legal guardian of the child shall make any financial claim against DONOR.

d)   If RECIPIENT should ever marry, DONOR and RECIPIENT agree that RECIPIENT's husband may adopt the child at RECIPIENT's sole discretion.

e)   RECIPIENT, in her sole discretion, may travel or reside with the child in any city or state or foreign country.

f)   If DONOR and RECIPIENT should remain friends and the child comes to know the DONOR, this shall not be considered as weakening this agreement in any way or as giving DONOR any parental obligation or responsibility.

Note: *These two kinds of agreements both pertain to a situation where the donor and recipient did not have a prior emotional involvement. In contrast, perhaps you have been involved with the father but the relationship has ended, and you and he have agreed that he will have some substantial involvement in your child's life. In such a situation you would be wise to draw up some kind of an agreement with him. The simplest way to do this would be to ask a lawyer to draw up a standard separation agreement for you just like he would for a divorcing couple.*

APPENDIX D

. . . .

SUPPORT GROUPS

In addition to these actual groups, if you have a computer and access to the Internet, there is a wealth of support and information available through the many virtual support groups for single parenting, fertility, adoption, and more.

Single Mothers by Choice
P.O. Box 1642
New York, NY 10028
(212) 988-0993
www.singlemothersbychoice.com
An organization with national membership that provides support and information on resources for single women who have either decided to become or are considering becoming single mothers by conception or adoption. They have local chapters that meet around the country and publish a quarterly newsletter and local membership directories. They also maintain a registry so mothers of children conceived by donor insemination can try to locate half-siblings. Call or write to request a free brochure about their services.

RESOLVE
7910 Woodmont Ave., Suite 1350
Bethesda, MD 20814
(301) 652-8585, (888) 623-0744
www.resolve.org
A national organization for couples and singles struggling with infertility. Has many publications and will refer you to local chapters. Excellent source of up-to-date information on fertility drugs and procedures. Also has support groups for infertile people who are trying to resolve their feelings about infertility and decide whether or not to adopt.

Parents Without Partners
1650 South Dixie Hwy #510
Boca Raton, FL 33432
(561) 391-8833
www.parentswithoutpartners.com
A self-help organization with activities for divorced, widowed, or never-married parents. They will refer you to local groups and organizations.

La Leche League International
P.O. Box 4079
Schaumburg, IL 60168
(800) LALECHE or (847) 519-7730
www.lalecheleague.org
An international volunteer organization with local chapters. They are experts on and advocates of breast-feeding and will refer you to local chapters that have support groups to help you solve any problems you may have with the process.

Family Pride Coalition
P.O. Box 65327
Washington, DC 20035

(202) 331-5015
www.familypride.org
Support and advocacy group for lesbian and gay parents and their children. Will refer you to local resources.

Momazons
P.O. Box 82069
Columbus, OH 43202
(614) 267-0193
An organization for lesbian mothers and for lesbians who want children in their lives. Services include a bimonthly newsletter and referrals to appropriate resources.

National Organization of Single Mothers (NOSM)
P.O. Box 68
Midland, NC 28107
(704) 888-KIDS
www.singlemothers.org
Publishes a bimonthly newsletter for divorced, widowed, and never-married mothers. Has local chapters.

Doulas of North America (DONA)
P.O. Box 626
Jasper, IN 47547
(888) 788-DONA
www.dona.org
National headquarters; call them for information of finding a doula (someone to act as a support person during the pregnancy, birth, and/or postpartum.)

BIG BROTHERS

Big Brothers/Big Sisters of America
230 North 13th Street
Philadelphia, PA 19107
(215) 567-7000
ww.bbbsa.org
Provides professionally supervised adult men and women to serve as role models for children from single-parent homes. They have local offices in many cities and are nondenominational. They usually give big brothers to boys, but regulations vary and in some cities a little girl *can* get a big brother, so ask your local resource if they would consider cross-gender matching.

Also check for denominational big brother organizations in your area, such as Jewish Big Brothers, Catholic Big Brothers, and the like.

RECOMMENDED READING

Please note that this is a very selective list. There are hundreds of books available on these subjects, but I have listed some of my personal favorites as well as those that members of the Single Mothers by Choice organization have liked and recommended. Some are quite old, but all are still in print. They are listed by topic.

ABOUT SINGLE PARENTS

Single by Chance, Mothers by Choice. Rosanna Hertz. Oxford Press, 2006. Thought-provoking stories of several women making the choice to become single moms.

The Complete Single Mother: Reassuring Answers to Your Most Challenging Concerns. Andrea Engber and Leah Klugness. Adams, 1995. An enjoyable book that really does live up to its subtitle. Has a special section for SMCs.

In Praise of Single Parents: Mothers and Fathers Embracing the Challenge. Shoshana Alexander. Houghton Mifflin, 1994. Mothers and fathers who were divorced, widowed, or who chose single parenthood talk about their experiences and how they cope. An inspiring book.

On Our Own: Unmarried Motherhood in America. Melissa Ludtke. Random House, 1997. A well-written, comprehensive, and thought-provoking overview of the whole subject.

The Single Mothers Companion: Essays and Stories by Women. Marsha Leslie (ed.). Seal Press, 1994. A collection that includes essays by both famous and unknown writers on subjects related to single motherhood. Many are moving; you may need a supply of tissues.

MAKING THE DECISION

Maybe Baby: 28 Writers Tell the Truth About Skepticism, Infertility, Baby Lust, Childlessness, Ambivalence, and How They Made the Biggest Decision of Their Lives. Lori Leibovich (ed.). HarperCollins, 2006. Exploration of the big decision—whether or not to have a child.

Choosing Single Motherhood: The Thinking Woman's Guide. Mikki Morrissette. Be-Mondo Publishing, 2006. For single women considering parenthood, as well as those who already have children.

INSEMINATION, INFERTILITY, AND NEW TECHNOLOGIES

Mommies, Daddies, Donors, Surrogates: Answering Tough Questions and Building Strong Families. Diane Ehrensaft, Ph.D. The Guilford Press, 2005. A wonderful book that addresses the complex issues which arise from choosing a nontraditional way to have a family. It is one of the few books that includes detailed and sound guidance for speaking with your child about these issues. A must-have.

The Infertility Cure: The Ancient Chinese Wellness Program for Getting Pregnant and Having Healthy Babies. Randine Lewis, Ph.D. Little, Brown and Company, 2005. Recommended for those who want to go beyond traditional medicine when trying to conceive.

Sweet Grapes: How to Stop Being Infertile and Start Living Again. Jean W. Carter and Michael Carter. Perspective Press, 1998.

Helping the Stork: The Choices and Challenges of Donor Insemination. Carol Frost Vercollone, M.S.W., Robert Moss, Ph.D., and Heidi Moss, M.S.W. Wiley, 1997. A consumer guide to donor insemination with practical information on medical and sperm bank options. An invaluable resource if you're considering insemination.

Taking Charge of Your Fertility. Toni Weschler, M.P.H. Harper Perennial, 1995. A thorough basic book.

Six Steps to Increased Fertility: An Integrated Medical and Mind/ Body Program to Promote Conception. Robert L. Barbieri, M.D., Alice D. Domar, Ph.D., and Kevin R. Loughlin, M.D. Simon & Schuster, 2001.

The Essential Guide to Lesbian Conception, Pregnancy, and Birth. Kim Toevs and Stephanie Brill. Alyson Publications, 2002. Not just for lesbians—it presents both the options and mechanics of alternative conception, as well as "thinking exercises" to work through preconceptions, biases, and concerns about getting to motherhood via a nontraditional path.

Lethal Secrets: The Shocking Consequences and Unsolved Problems of Artificial Insemination. Annette Baran and Reuben Pannor. Warner Books, 1989. Presents a strong argument for openness about a child's origins.

Having Your Baby by Donor Insemination. Elizabeth Noble. Houghton Mifflin, 1987. An informative guidebook, dated medically (it was written pre-AIDS) but particularly good on the subject of insemination by a known donor.

PREGNANCY

The Everything Getting Pregnant Book: Professional, Reassuring Advice to Help You Conceive. Robin Elise Weiss. Adams, 2004. Covers all the basics about getting pregnant.

Mothering the New Mother: Women's Feelings and Needs After Childbirth. Sally Placksin. Newmarket Press, 2000. A wise and delightful book for any new mother about the postpartum and post-adoptive period.

When Pregnancy Isn't Perfect. Laurie A Rich. Larata Press, 1996. Everything from constant morning sickness to C-section to preemies. A nice review.

Two of Us Make a World: The Single Mother's Guide to Pregnancy, Birth, and the First Year. Prudence and Sherrill Tippins. Henry Holt, 1996. Mostly focused on pregnancy, the introduction alone (by Anne Lamott) is worth the price of the book.

Manual of High Risk Pregnancy and Delivery. Elizabeth Stepp Gilbert, R.N.C., M.S., and Judith Smith Harmon, R.N., M.S. Mosby, 1993. If you, like many "older" mothers, are having a high risk pregnancy/delivery, this book is a very comprehensive guide to assist you.

What to Expect When You're Expecting. Arlene Eisenberg, Heidi Eisenberg Murkoff, and Sandee Eisenberg Hathaway, R.N. Workman Publishing, 1991. These three women answer the big and little questions of pregnancy. Also, *What to Expect the First Year* by the same authors is another well-respected book.

A Child is Born. Lennart Nilsson. Delacorte Press, 1990.

Detailed actual photographs of the development of the embryo inside the womb during pregnancy. Incredible.

ADOPTION

Adopting on Your Own: The Complete Guide to Adopting as a Single Parent. Lee Varon. Farrar, Straus and Giroux, 2000. Written by a counselor and single adoptive mother, this book covers the issues thoroughly and well.

The Complete Adoption Book: Everything You Need to Know to Adopt a Child. Laura Beauvais-Godwin and Raymond Godwin. Adams Media, 2005. They are a husband and wife who adopted domestically, and he is an adoption attorney. The book includes information on international adoption but is probably best as a resource on domestic adoption. There's a state-by-state summary of adoption laws in the appendix as well as a list of agencies and attorneys by state.

Cross Cultural Adoption: How to Answer Questions from Family, Friends and Community. Amy Coughlin and Caryn Abramowitz. LifeLine Press, 2004.

Toddler Adoption: The Weaver's Craft. Mary Hopkins-Best. Perspective Press, 1998. The book deals primarily with adopting one- to three-year-olds. Addresses a lot of the potential problems adoptive parents may face when adopting children at this age, including attachment disorder, and ways to overcome them.

Launching a Baby's Adoption. Patricia Irwin Johnston. Tapestry Books, 1997. A guidebook that examines the many issues involved in preparing for adoptive parenthood and for that all-important first year.

The Adoption Reader: Birth Mothers, Adoptive Mothers, and Adopted Daughters Tell Their Stories. Susan Wadia-Ellis (ed.). Seal Press, 1995. Emotional stories of adoption from all parts of the adoption scenario. A rich conversation.

Being Adopted: A Lifelong Search for Self. David Brodzinski, Marshall Schecter, and Robin Henig. Doubleday, 1992. One of the best books about the emotional impact of adoption.

Making Sense of Adoption: A Parent's Guide. Lois Melina. Harper Perennial, 1989. Not just about adoption, this is relevant also to children of any alternative means of conception. A guide to helping your child, at all different ages and stages, to under-stand his or her unique story. One of the few books with use-ful ideas about how to talk to a child about adoption and donor insemination.

The Adoption Resource Book. Lois Gilman. Harper Perennial, 1992. One of the most comprehensive and useful books on adoption for those getting oriented to the adoption world.

CHILD DEVELOPMENT AND CHILD REARING

Raising Your Spirited Child. Mary Sheedy Kurcinka. Harper Paperbacks, 2006. She also wrote another book called *Kids, Parents, and Power Struggles.* Help with teaching kids how to handle their emotions and basing discipline on underlying feelings. Also has a whole section on parents dealing with their own emotions.

How to Talk So Kids Will Listen and Listen So Kids Will Talk. Adele Faber and Elaine Mazlish. Collins, 20th anniversary ed., 2004.

Emotional Life of the Toddler. Alicia F. Lieberman. Free Press, 1995. A very valuable guide to understanding and dealing with the often-frustrating toddler.

Oneness and Separateness: From Infant to Individual. Louis J. Kaplan, Ph.D. Simon & Schuster, 1995. A lyrically written description of the infant's "second birth," the birth of his/her unique psychological self during the first three years. An all-time favorite of mine.

Your Child's Emotional Health: The Early Years. Philadelphia Child Guidance Center. Macmillan, 1994. This is just one in a good series of books from this source for sound advice on child development.

Mom, There's a Man in the Kitchen and He's Wearing Your Robe: The Single Mother's Guide to Dating Well Without Parenting Poorly. Ellie Slott Fisher. DeCapo Press, 2005.

The Lesbian and Gay Parenting Handbook. April Martin, Ph.D. Harper Perennial, 1993. Addresses the particular concerns of gay and lesbian parents, but would be helpful to anyone trying to be the best parent they can be.

Love and Anger: The Parental Dilemma. Nancy Samalin. Penguin Books, 1992. An excellent approach to discipline that respects both parent and child. Also by Nancy Samalin: *Loving Your Child Is Not Enough.*

Making Sense of Adoption: A Parent's Guide. Lois Melina. Harper Perennial, 1989. Not just about adoption, this is relevant also to children of any alternative means of conception. A guide to helping your child, at all different ages and stages, to understand his or her unique story. One of the few books with useful ideas about how to talk to a child about adoption and donor insemination.

Your Baby and Child: From Birth to Age Five. Penelope Leach, M.D. Alfred A. Knopf, Revised edition, 1997. Often called the "new

Dr. Spock," Leach mixes the practical and the psychological in readable books. Also by Leach: *The First Six Months*. A guide through the earliest, and for many the most difficult, stage of motherhood.

Babies and Their Mothers. D. W. Winnicott. Addison-Wesley Publishing Co., 1988. Winnicott understands babies (and mothers) in a rare way. This book is a special one.

A Good Enough Parent. Bruno Bettelheim. Vintage, 1988. A thoughtful and thought-provoking examination of parenting.

RAISING BOYS

Raising Boys Without Men: How Maverick Moms Are Creating the Next Generation of Exceptional Men. Peggy Drexler, Ph.D., with Linden Gross. Rodale Books, 2005. Very well done and reassuring discussion of the issues.

Raising Cain: Protecting the Emotional Life of Boys. Dan Kindlon, Ph.D., and Michael Thompson, Ph.D. Ballantine Books, 2000. Provides understanding and insights on the inner life of boys from birth through the college years.

The Courage to Raise Good Men. Olga Silverstein. Penguin, 1995. An outstanding guide for mothers of sons by a very wise family therapist.

FOR THE CHILDREN

It's So Amazing! Robie H. Harris. Candlewick Press, 2004. This is a great book about body parts, puberty, and how babies are made and born. It talks about adoption, insemination, and IVF in very easy terms that children can understand

The Family Book. Todd Parr. Megan Tingley Books, 2003.

When Mama Comes Home Tonight. Eileen Spinelli. Little Simon, 2001.

I Love You Like Crazy Cakes. Rose A. Lewis. Little, Brown and Company, 2000. A children's book written by and about a single mom who adopted from China.

The Best Single Mom in the World: How I Was Adopted. Mary Zisk. Albert Whitman & Company, 2001. A single mother's story of adopting.

My Mother and Me: A Memory Scrapbook for Kids. Kids Can Press, 2000. No mention of a dad and includes a family tree to fill out without the dad's side. www.kidscanpress.com.

I Love You the Purplest. Barbara M. Joosse. Chronicle Books, 1996. For preschoolers—the story of a single mother of two boys.

One Hundred Is a Family. Paul Munoz Ryan. Hyperion, 1996. A counting book in rhyme that uses different kinds of families to illustrate the numbers. A neat way to make the point without preaching.

When You Were Born in China: A Memory Book for Children Adopted from China. Sara Dorrow, 1996. This is a unique and highly recommended book which you can order from the publisher Brian Boyd at Yeong and Yeong Books, 1368 Michelle Drive, St. Paul, MN 55123. It is really a book for older children, nine and up. (If you write "FCC" on your order, a portion of the proceeds will go to Families with Children from China [FCC]. The price is $18.50 including shipping.)

A Mother for Choco. Keiko Kaska. Paper Star, 1996. Choco is a little bird in search of a mother who looks just like him. When Mrs. Bear takes him in he realizes that a mother is someone who loves and cares for you, not someone who looks like you. Ideal for those who are raising a child from a different racial or ethnic background.

Do I Have a Daddy? Jeanne Warren Lindsay. Morning Glory Press, 1992. A sensitive picture book about a young child who asks his mother about the father he has never known. Useful in helping to broach the subject and includes a valuable section for parents.

Mama, Do You Love Me? Barbara Joosse. Scholastic Books, 1992. This book is a classic about anger and unconditional love, beautifully illustrated with watercolors depicting an Inuit mother and daughter.

Families are Different. Nina Pellegrini. Holiday House, 1991. The book is told from the point of view of an adopted girl. For kindergarten through first grade. This book explains that "family" is a bond created more by love than by biological relationships.

INDEX

of donor insemination, 36–38
father described to, *see* daddy
  issue
father's involvement with, 41, 50,
  54
feelings of, 19, 36–37, 125
genetic endowment of, 64–65, 74,
  77–78
identification by, 173–74
importance of man in life of,
  162–76
inner reality of, 138, 197
legal guardian of, 103, 104–5, 189
as link to father, 54
nurturing of, 20, 79, 135, 162
rights of, 25–26, 45, 181, 184–85
role model for, 163–66, 171–73
search for biological parents by,
  74–77
and secrets, 148–49
and sense of identity, 76
and SMC-father relationship,
  53–54
and SMC's dating, 194–202
and SMC's ex-boyfriend, 200–201
trauma to, 18–20, 79
and unknown donor, 185–86
world viewed by, 146–48
childbirth classes, 104, 109
child care, books about, 232
child development issues, 160–79
  and adoption, 78
  books about, 228–30
  discipline, 176–79
  importance of men, 162–76
  separation, 161–62
child support:
  as child's right, 25–26, 45, 181
  and paternal rights, 181, 183, 185
  and public assistance, 184
closed adoption, vs. open adoption,
  70–77, 84
coach, labor, 103–4, 106, 108

college fund, 21
communication:
  child-father, 31, 34–35, 155, 159
  with doctor, 29
  in open adoption, 71–77, 84
  with other new mothers, 108–9
conception, 24–60
  and age, 27–28
  by donor insemination, 26–30
  with partner, 45–59
  and sex, 40
contract, with sperm bank, 31, 33
coparenting:
  agreement about, 50–51, 55, 181
  as child's right, 25–26, 181
  as father's right, 42, 181
  feelings about, 50–52
  questions about, 41
  vs. single motherhood, 4
cost:
  of adoption, 62
  of insemination, 28
counseling:
  about adoption, 70
  about relationship, 53–54
  of couple, 48, 51–52, 55
  and daddy issue, 130
"couple friends," 192
custody:
  and adoptive mother, 188–89
  as father's right, 42, 113, 182

daddy issue, 122–59
  and alternative family, 124–25
  books about, 232
  and child's feelings, 125, 142
  and demographics, 125
  empathy in, 142–43
  and family, 127–29
  father's role in, 126–27, 148–49,
    156
  five/six-year-old's questions on,
    144–49

ABOUT THE AUTHOR

JANE MATTES, LCSW, BCD, has had her
own psychotherapy practice in New York
City for over twenty years. To write this
book she has drawn on her extensive professional counseling experience, her close
contact with hundreds of members of the
Single Mothers By Choice organization,
which she founded in 1981 and still di-
rects, and her personal experience as the
single mother of an adult son.